THE GOD WHO SPEAKS

author
Sister Eileen Wheeler

Published by The Reverend Eileen Wheeler

Printed by The Printing Place Ltd
Chelmsford, Essex
www.printingplace.co.uk

ISBN 0-9539449-0-5

© Eileen Wheeler 2000

No part of this publication may be reproduced by any means whatsoever without the prior permission of the author.

Front and Back Cover:
The background to the cover depicts the restored Coach House in the Manor Gardens, Bexhill. The Servants with Jesus have provided this resource as a place of quiet, refreshment and help for the local community. The two insets on the front cover portray the Prayer Garden gateway and fountain.

This book is dedicated in memory of my parents Austin and Violet Wheeler

Most of the Scripture quotations are from the Revised Standard Version of the Bible. Other quotations are from the Authorized Version.

Contents

Foreword i
Sketch map of East Sussex ii
Introduction and acknowlegements iii
1. Getting to Know Jesus 1
2. Seeking the Spirit 4
3. Called to spread the Good News 9
4. Testing the Call 17
5. Commissioned to Serve in East Sussex 23
6. Out and About in East Sussex 25
7. Surprises! 31
8. The Vision for the Servants with Jesus 41
9. Sharing the Vision 44
10. Planning for the Future 49
11. Working, Watching and Waiting 57
12. Continuing to Work, Watch and Wait 65
13. Action for Restoration 71
14. Marvellous Provision 79
15. Taking our Stand in Jerusalem 87
16. Living in Jerusalem 103
17. God's Workers 111
18. Hospice Preparations 115
19. Living in No-man's-land 123
20. New Beginnings 129
21. Released to be a Deacon 135
22. God's Secret Plans 141
23. Growth and Expansion 147
24. Journey into Priesthood 155
25. Fulfilment 161
26. Aspirations for the Future 169
    Epilogue 173

Foreword

I cannot say that I know Bexhill particularly well. Indeed I am never quite sure where it begins and where it ends. Such places as Cooden, Bexhill, St Leonards, Hastings and Ore represent a prolonged blur of the southern coastline whenever I have driven from Eastbourne to Dungeness for a holiday outing. Nor do I know Eileen Wheeler particularly well, except that we were in the Cambridge Christian Union together in the late 40s and 50s and only met again at a "Fifty Years on" reunion a year ago. But the story she has written I have found compelling reading.

It tells of one person's vision and experience of God. It can not help being autobiographical (indeed that is what makes it such a good read), but it is really a story of what God has been doing in the lives of a whole group of people and what He has done through them. It tells of numbers of young people giving themselves to the service of God and we rather wish that the author could have broken a few confidences and told us how they have gone on in their Christian discipleship. It tells of a handful of mature Christian women banding themselves together in a growing fellowship of prayer and service under the title of Servants with Jesus. It tells of the birth of a hospice and the establishing of a place of prayer and sanctuary in the heart of Bexhill. It has its fair share of struggles and agonisings. It is not all plain sailing by any means. It tells of sometimes astonishing answers to prayer. In a word, it tells of a great God at work in a small southern coastal town.

That is its fascination. Local people who know several of the names will read it with special interest. Quite apart from its intrinsic value to the churches of Bexhill and district, it represents an important slice of local history too that needs to have been written. And others like me who come from further afield will read it as a remarkable chronicle of what has happened over several years in a part of East Sussex where God's Spirit has been listened to and obeyed.

The sceptic may wonder about the validity of the visions that inspired the work. The cynic may ask all kinds of questions that are not answered in these pages: Where did all the money come from? What were the underlying motives behind these remarkable women? What is happening to them all today? Is this same God still at work in Bexhill, and if so, how? But most readers, I feel sure, will react as I have done and say simply "Glory be to God on high" over an enthralling story told with engaging modesty and charm.

John B Taylor, Bishop of St Albans (1980-95)

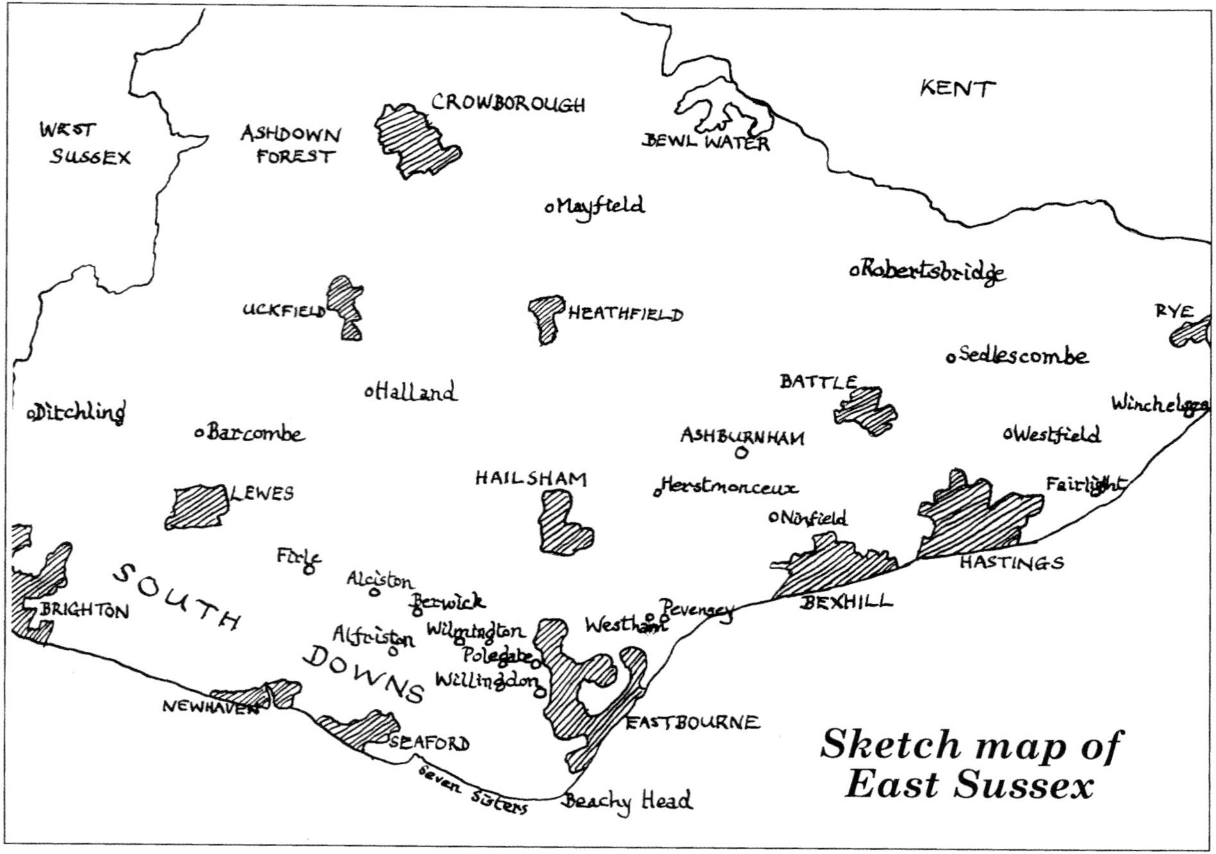

Sketch map of East Sussex

Introduction

In the mid-sixties, God broke into my world in new ways. He was very present. I discovered that He could be known intimately in everyday life. Others too, were experiencing the reality of His presence.

I began to keep a detailed diary of thanksgivings, events and insights given by the Spirit.

Over the years people whom I respect, have suggested I write a book about those early years and the history of the Servants with Jesus. I have always resisted this, feeling that many things that happen between God and His people, are secret and should stay that way.

Last summer I was urged by Deborah Scott-Bromley, the news editor of the Bexhill Observer, our local newspaper, to write. She was very definite that the history of the things the Lord had done among us in Bexhill and the surrounding East Sussex area should not be lost.

My prayer is that all who read this book will understand that God speaks and see that He is at work today. It is not the privilege of a spiritual elite to hear God. He longs to communicate with everyone He has created. He wants us to know Him in our daily lives.

Many people have contributed to the production of this book. In particular I would like to thank Deborah Scott-Bromley, who has used her expertise to comment helpfully on each chapter. I would also like to thank Mary-Joan Lloyd who has given invaluable help in listening, making constructive criticisms and in typing. I appreciate the help given in reading the proofs by Pat Freeman, a friend of my brother from the Old Chelmsfordians, who is himself a writer. I should like to thank Carl Copsey of Peter Reed Printers Ltd, Chelmsford, for his encouragement and co-operation. Without his suggestions, this book would not have been produced.

I decided to dedicate the book to my parents. Although I begin this story in my mid-thirties and do not write much about my childhood days, my parents were responsible for the foundations of my formation. My mother was entirely motivated by a desire to make others happy. My father's motivation can be summed up in some words from Shakespeare's Hamlet:

"This above all: to thine own self be true;
And it must follow as the night the day,
Thou canst not then be false to any man."

Before the story begins, I include the encouraging comments of two East Sussex church leaders.

The Bible contains many instances when the divine Word is spoken. Like Samuel, we are not ready to listen! We are also surprised at the clear memory of those who hear and respond. We learn the importance of being still and silent in our times of meditation. Today we discover these truths anew. We are on a steep 'learning curve'. How grateful then to those who help us in this process. This book guides us forward.

Michael Townroe, Rector of Bexhill (1959-82)
and Rural Dean of Battle and Bexhill

A challenging collection of amazing coincidences or miraculous occurences carefully chosen to point the reader in the direction of the God who speaks.

When Eileen Wheeler gave up a promising career in obedience to God's call more than a few eyebrows were raised in the sitting rooms of East Sussex. The formation of Servants with Jesus, clothed in a distinctive purple, led to all sorts of rumours ranging from 'an order of married nuns' to 'a breakaway church'.

Undoutedly misunderstanding remains- often among those who have not had the opportunity to weigh the evidence- but through Servants with Jesus Christian women, married, single, divorced and widowed, have found productive ways to proclaim the unity of the people of God to a degree that has often eluded male church leaders.

Servants with Jesus has never been a large group but continues to be a valued prophetic symbol of what bridge building can achieve.

Eileen's struggle towards ordination as a priest in the Anglican church is related with graciousness and charity, giving valuable insights as to how those with differing views have endeavoured to remain in fellowship with each other.

After more than 30 years of praying, Sister Eileen still anticipates Revival in East Sussex. Maybe the 21st century will see Servants with Jesus receiving its first members from the Roman Catholic church, thus restoring the unity among Christian women to a level not seen since the Reformation.

Dennis Nolan, Pastor, Battle Baptist Church
and Chairman of Trustees, Servants with Jesus

Chapter One

Getting to Know Jesus

"He shall see of the travail of His soul and shall be satisfied." Isaiah 53:11

" Revival has broken out in Bexhill! You had better go and tell the Rector!"
This was the Reverend John Bickersteth's response to all I shared with him over breakfast one Monday morning in February 1965. Numbers of young women and girls had just come to new faith and new birth.

At the time I was headmistress of the Bexhill Grammar School for Girls. I was staying at Ashburnham Place for the weekend with about sixty of the senior girls and a few members of staff. We had come together to learn more about the Christian faith. Our speakers were the Reverend Christopher Steer, a Baptist Minister from Bexley and Doctor Marguerite von Bergen, an old university friend of mine, who was home on furlough from Burundi.

On Saturday morning before breakfast, I began to read the scripture verses set for the day in the devotional book Daily Light. The first words I read spoke to me powerfully. God Himself was speaking to me through the scriptures. The words were from the old Authorised Version of the Book of Isaiah: "He shall see the travail of His soul and shall be satisfied." Isaiah 53:11. I had an instant conviction that something very special was going to happen during the weekend - something that would give pleasure to God's heart.

Throughout Saturday and most of Sunday the programme proceeded much as at previous weekends. There were stimulating talks and discussions in the Library. The girls enjoyed being together and revelled in the beautiful surroundings and the good meals!

On Saturday evening, Marguerite showed slides of her hospital work and shared moving testimonies of some of her African friends and staff. Some of her helpers were refugees who had fled over the border from Rwanda during times of tribal trouble and conflict. One man was praising God, because by being a refugee, he had come to know Jesus. Marguerite also read a letter she had received from her friend Mary, a widow, whose husband, Pastor Yona, had been murdered in the troubles. Mary shared how, though she missed Yona very much, she had felt closer to Jesus than ever before. She had come to know Him as a friend and companion in her daily life. The slides and testimonies made a strong and indelible impression.

On the Sunday evening Christopher was leading the meeting. Before giving the talk, he gave a simple directive. He suggested that no one should go home the next day, without seeking to have their questions answered. He invited everyone to take the opportunity at the end of the meeting to either talk to one of the speakers, a member of staff or one of their Christian friends. There was no emotional pressure of any kind, just an offer to talk. Christopher's straightforward remark was used to release people to communicate and to talk about Jesus in a totally natural way. The burning questions were, "How can I know God? How can I know Jesus?" Talking went on well into the night. Numbers of girls came to Christian faith and to know Jesus and God the Father personally. Lasting and transforming relationships with the Lord were made and established. I do not know to this day how many were converted. What I do know is that God the Holy Spirit took the initiative. He drew people into a new relationship with Himself, with God as Heavenly Father and with Jesus as Saviour and Lord.

The next morning we met in the Library before breakfast for the usual school-type of prayers; that is a hymn, scripture reading and prayer. A member of staff was leading the short service and suggested that, after the hymn and reading and before the formal prayers, there should be a pause when anyone could offer their own prayers of thanksgiving. To my shame, my immediate reaction was one of embarrassment. "No one will take part!" was my thought. To my amazement about forty people spontaneously made short prayers of thanksgiving from all round the room. We then went into the Oak Dining Room for breakfast. It worked out that Marguerite and I sat next to John Bickersteth.

In those days, I did not know John well. Most of us stood in awe of him. After all, he had inherited the home of the previous Earls of Ashburnham! We felt privileged that he always welcomed us personally to Ashburnham and also found time to meet with us in the Library on Friday evenings, to tell us something of the history of Ashburnham and his vision for the future. Marguerite and I shared with him the happenings of the previous evening and described what had taken place in the Library before breakfast. He instantly recognised a special work of God the Holy Spirit, containing the seeds of Revival. He knew it was important that I shared with the Rector of Bexhill what had taken place. It was not until that moment that I realised the magnitude of all that had happened amongst us. The Lord had indeed fulfilled the promise He made to me on Saturday morning. He had seen of the travail of His soul and been satisfied.

Canon Michael Townroe was the Rector of Bexhill at the time, and also our Chairman of Governors. Later on Monday, Marguerite and I went to visit

Michael, to share with him what had taken place during the weekend. He recognised a real work of God and was keen for its effect to spill over into the whole neighbourhood. "We need a Cell Movement, something like we had in the war" he said. "We need to make it possible for small prayer and study groups to take place throughout the area, for mutual support." Michael suggested that these should take place as far as possible in the homes of the girls, so that parents could become involved. Under this umbrella, groups emerged in Bexhill, Ashburnham, Willingdon, Hailsham, the Battle area and Robertsbridge.

The events of February 1965 proved to be the beginning of a remarkable work of the Spirit of God in the whole area surrounding Bexhill. At the Grammar School we had four successive Christian head girls and there was a continuous stream of conversions. I recently met an old girl of the school and asked her what the girls talked about in those days. Her answer was immediate, "How can we know Jesus?" From time to time I continued to talk with Michael Townroe and John Bickersteth. I also exchanged news with the Reverend Edmund Heddle, who was Minister of Beulah Baptist Church, Bexhill and a Governor of the Grammar School. It was clear that the Spirit of God was at work in the lives of a significant number of adults. Christians were being renewed and some were being brought to faith for the first time. A promise of the Lord from the Book of Isaiah seemed to aptly describe what was taking place:

"I will pour water on the thirsty land and streams on the dry ground; I will pour My Spirit upon your descendants and My blessing on your offspring. They shall spring up like grass amid waters, like willows by flowing streams. This one will say, 'I am the Lord's'.......and another will write on his hand, 'The Lord's'." Isaiah 44:3-5.

Chapter Two

Seeking the Spirit

"But you shall receive power when the Holy Spirit has come upon you; and you shall be My witnesses." Acts 1:8

"You are not concentrating Miss Wheeler! You're behaving as though you are in love!" The deputy head was speaking to me while we were working together on a new school timetable. She was right. Many things had happened to me since the weekend away at Ashburnham. A year and a half had passed and I had a new relationship of love with the Lord and with His people.

During the weeks that followed our visit to Ashburnham, I began to reread the New Testament from a different perspective, giving special attention to the passages about the Holy Spirit. I was surprised at the numerous occasions His activity was mentioned. It was difficult to understand how previously I had not noticed this fact. Also, I had not fully grasped the vital part He had taken in the spreading of the Christian Gospel.

In the past my thinking had concentrated on the love of God the Father in sending His Son Jesus Christ to die for our sins and to rise again to give us eternal life. I believed in the Holy Spirit, but as a rather background influence, who mysteriously guided us and kept us from harm. I had been brought up in a flourishing Congregational Church, where we were taught that the Holy Spirit guided the Church and helped Christians to make the right decisions. I had known His directive in some of the major decisions in my life. Naturally, I was of a rather fearful nature, so I had often prayed that some words of St. Paul would be true for me: "God has not given us the Spirit of fear, but of power, and love, and of a sound mind" 2 Timothy 1:7.

In 1957 I had been confirmed in St. Alban's Abbey at the age of twenty-eight. At that time I had come to see that the laying-on-of-hands was one of the Biblical outward signs for receiving the blessing of the Holy Spirit. In spite of all my head knowledge about the Spirit and the various steps I had taken over the years, I knew I had not experienced the release and freedom enjoyed by the first disciples. I did not possess their confidence and assurance of faith. I did not have the boldness they possessed after they had been baptised in the Spirit on the Day of Pentecost. I therefore resolved to seek earnestly for this baptism of love and power.

During the Easter holidays I was given a book to read called The Cross and the Switchblade. It was about an American country minister who had been convicted about wasting too much time watching television. He decided, instead of viewing, to spend one to two hours each evening praying. Directly as a result of this, he was led by the Holy Spirit into an extraordinarily successful work amongst the teenage gangs and drug addicts of New York. During October, Michael Townroe wrote a most challenging pastoral letter in the St. Peter's parish magazine. He asked all of us in his congregation to pray for Revival beginning with ourselves. So, bearing in mind the story of the Cross and the Switchblade, I began in the evenings to give some of my television viewing time to doing what the Rector had asked us to do.

One evening in November, I prayed specifically to be filled with the Holy Spirit. I asked the Lord to show me if there was anything in my life preventing me from receiving all His blessings or any step of obedience I needed to take. As I prayed a picture came into my mind of a pool of water. On either side of the pool stood two Baptist ministers. One was Edmund Heddle, the other the Minister of Sidley Baptist Church, David Jones, who had been instrumental in numbers of young people coming to Christian faith. Edmund and David were the only two people I knew personally who had received the Holy Spirit in the way described in the Acts of the Apostles. In the picture they were both pointing into the pool of water. The interpretation was clear. The Holy Spirit appeared to be speaking about baptism by immersion. This thought came to me as a great surprise. Nothing else tangible happened at the moment of asking. There was no emotional experience or any other manifestation of the gifts of the Spirit.

Since the Ashburnham weekend I had kept in close contact with Michael Townroe. In the light of his earlier encouragement to pray for Revival, it was natural to share with Michael what had taken place. He was always a good listener and weighed things carefully and sensitively. He recognised that God the Holy Spirit was working in my life and circumstances, but baptism by immersion after confirmation did not fit into his theology. He suggested that prayer with anointing with oil might be more appropriate as it was a Biblical ordinance for those dedicating their lives to the service of God. This, to me, did not seem to be the course of action indicated by the picture I had been given. For the time being we left things as they were and agreed to continue in prayer.

Within a few days it was evident that the Holy Spirit had begun to work within me in gentle and wonderful ways, meeting me at the point of my deepest needs.

First, I experienced a marvellous miracle of healing. At the age of nineteen I began to suffer from a condition known as premature menopause. Doctors and Specialists were unable to help me. It will not take much imagination to realise how much distress this caused me throughout my twenties and thirties. I knew that if I married I would be unlikely to have children. At the age of thirty-two I was appointed as headmistress of the Bexhill Girls' Grammar School. I decided to lay aside any thought of marriage. The Lord had given me approximately four hundred and fifty girls and thirty members of staff to look after. Quite a family! I decided to put all my energies into caring for their welfare. This I did to the best of my ability. It was an amazing surprise to discover a few years later, at the age of thirty-seven, that I had been totally healed. I never looked back. The disability was completely removed. I seemed to be a new and different person.

Secondly, I had a changed relationship with God as Father and with Jesus His Son. I came to know them more intimately in my daily life. As I read the Bible, they seemed to be speaking to me directly. Verses of scripture came alive with an immediate and relevant meaning. Prayer took on a new dimension and was no longer such an effort and dull discipline. A deepening awareness of God's love often turned prayer into worship. I knew with a sure certainty that: "nothing would be able to separate me from the love of God that is in Christ Jesus our Lord" Romans 8:39.

Thirdly, my relationships with others changed. People around me began to feel a warmth and love coming from me that had not been experienced before. I was unaware of this myself until comments were made. For example a member of staff stopped me in the corridor one day and said, "I am finding school prayers much more helpful these days". "In what way?" I asked. "There is much more warmth and reality in what you say" was the answer. A parent came to ask for help because her daughter was out of control. As we talked she suddenly said, "You love my daughter, don't you?" My answer was "Yes", but I did not realise this was so until the question had been asked. Sometime later the deputy head made her teasing and discerning remark.

At this time when so much was happening, I shared a home with some older Christian friends, Will and Vi Sidnell. They were like second parents. They were a tower of strength and I knew prayed for me frequently. They were active members of Beulah Baptist Church. We enjoyed good fellowship and often prayed together. One morning in December, I was preparing to leave them to drive to Chelmsford to spend Christmas with my own parents. I had loaded my car and then went to my bedroom to pray before setting out on the journey. I was very tired after an exhausting term. I can remember kneeling and praying earnestly for the Spirit to come and renew me, refresh me and release me so that I would be able to meet all the demands of the Christmas holidays.

Immediately there came into my mind thoughts from St. Paul's letter to the Ephesians: "Be filled with the Spirit....singing and making melody in your heart to the Lord" Ephesians 5:19. I knew the Lord was giving me the gift of singing in tongues and that I was to use this gift as I set out on my travels. I sang in tongues quietly most of the way to Chelmsford. It was not an ecstatic experience, but rather a matter of exercising my will to sing the words that were forming. Concentrating on the driving required me to be 'down to earth'! I even wondered whether I was making everything up but persisted in obedience to the instruction I had been given. On arrival I had a lovely confirmation of the genuineness of all that had happened. As I entered the kitchen door my Mother said, "Whatever has happened to you? You look so 'look-alive'!"

She was used to me arriving home tired at the end of term. The one who knew me better than anyone else knew that something special had happened to me.

Earlier in 1965 I had received an invitation to speak at the Bexhill Womens' World Day of Prayer, to be held at Sackville Road Methodist church in 1966. The theme set was: "You are My Witnesses" Isaiah 43:10. With such a theme it seemed obvious to recount something of the events of the previous year. I described how the Holy Spirit had changed lives, including my own. I shared how the Spirit had enabled us to know the Lord more intimately and to be better witnesses to Him. I reminded them how the witness of the Early Church, filled with the Holy Spirit had: "turned the world upside down". I then went on to challenge the women of Bexhill, "What about Bexhill in 1966? Do we expect God the Holy Spirit to work in power through the lives of Bexhill Christians?.......Let us pray continually that God, through His Holy Spirit, will transform all His people in this town into effective witnesses to His works of grace! May there be a mighty wind of the Spirit here in Bexhill!"

As 1966 progressed the idea began to develop that the Lord had a new calling for me for the future. There was a slow, but increasing conviction that one day I would leave the Grammar School to take up a wider ministry. In what capacity I had no idea. As the days passed I could not get out of my mind the earlier instruction to be baptised by immersion. It seemed this was a step of obedience that needed to be taken before the future would unfold. I went to share these thoughts with Michael. When he knew that this step of baptism was for me a matter of obedience, he said that I had no option but to obey. So I was baptised with Michael's blessing. I remember him saying at the time, "You are a High Church Baptist! You take the sacraments seriously!" I understood his insights and meaning. They were thought-provoking as I had been brought up in a tradition where sacraments had a low priority compared to the preaching of the Word. A few months later I was welcomed into the fellowship of Beulah Baptist Church. Neither Michael, Edmund nor I understood God's purpose in taking these steps. Michael shared an analogy, which I had not heard before. "God is weaving a tapestry. At present we are standing at the back of it and can see many loose ends. One day we will stand in front and see God's perfect pattern".

Chapter Three

Called to Spread the Good News

"How beautiful are the feet of those who bring good news!" Romans 10:15

I was twelve years old and it was the school holidays in August 1940. I was staying with my grandparents in Sudbury, Suffolk, when we received the news that a bomb had dropped in the garden next door to my parents' home in Chelmsford. No one had been killed or injured. We lived at number two in a semi-detached house. The bomb had dropped in the space between number four and number six.

At 5.55 pm on 19th August, my younger brother had set out on his bicycle to meet my father, returning from his work in London. He had cycled only a short distance when he looked up and saw a German bomber overhead. He returned quickly to the house to tell my mother. On arrival there was a screaming whistle and a bang. They both dived under the dining room table for shelter. My brother tells me that the bang was followed by a deathly silence, broken by the words, "This is the six o'clock news!" I can remember, on hearing about this, feeling very awed that no one had been hurt and that everyone was safe. As I gradually took in the news I had a strong sense of God's presence and protection. Although, at that point in time, I did not fully understand what it meant to be a Christian, I committed my life to God to use in whatever way He chose.

When I returned to school in September, we had a new Scripture teacher with a strong personal faith. She started a lively Christian discussion group. From time to time she invited interesting speakers to talk about their belief and Christian experiences. So I came to understand that the heart of Christian belief was about the love of God made known in Jesus Christ. A new birth and a new life were possible by welcoming Him into our lives and receiving the forgiveness He offered through dying on the Cross. By the age of fifteen, I had become a committed Christian.

Another strong influence in my teenage years was a young peoples' group, connected with the local Congregational churches. We went away together for study and fellowship weekends. In 1944 some of us took part in a week's conference at Cambridge, organised by the London Missionary Society.

During this week, I listened to an inspiring sermon based on a text from St. Paul's Letter to the Christians in Rome: "How are they to believe in Him of Whom they have never heard? And how are they to hear without a preacher?" Romans 10:14. Through these words I was called to spend my life sharing the Good News of Jesus with those who did not know Him. In those days the majority of people did not give a thought to the possibility of women being ordained and it was certainly not on my agenda! The obvious way to respond to the call was to go abroad as a missionary. With this in view, I started to train as a teacher at Homerton College, Cambridge, in September 1946.

Three significant things happened while I was at Homerton, which were to shape my future. One was the Cambridge Womens' Inter-Collegiate Christian Union or CWICCU, as it was known. Belonging to this society was a stimulating growth experience for a naturally shy and reserved person. Personal evangelism was high on the list of priorities, both during term time and vacations. We were encouraged to spend several weeks in the summer helping with children's beach missions. I spent two action-packed, happy summers helping with missions at Perranporth, in Cornwall. This was for me a confidence-building operation of sizeable proportions.

Secondly, the physical disability, described in the last chapter, began to develop during my second year of training. Sadly this involved me in missing several weeks of college life to see doctors and specialists.

Thirdly, for my finals in Divinity, I undertook some individual Biblical research about the Day of the Lord in the Old Testament and the Second Coming in the New Testament. The examiner expressed considerable interest in my work and as a result, I was offered a place at Newnham College to study for a degree in Theology. I taught for a year in a Secondary Modern School. I then had the privilege of returning to Cambridge for another three years' study.

By the time I returned to Cambridge, women had been admitted to full membership of the university. For the next three years, there were two main influences which shaped my thinking for the future. One was CICCU, which in 1948 had permitted women to become fully participating members for the first time. The other was Michael Ramsey, who, in 1950, became the Regius Professor of Divinity.

I was actively involved in the life of the CICCU, serving on the missionary committee and later as chairman of the womens' colleges' committee. There must have been three to four hundred members of the Christian Union in those days. We enjoyed a dynamic corporate prayer life. Evangelistic outreach into the university was effective and fruitful. High profile was given to serving God overseas. Numbers of students from that generation became well-known Christian leaders. Many others served God in full-time ministry, both in the United Kingdom and abroad.

New Testament lectures in the Divinity School, by Professor Michael Ramsey, were brilliant and prophetic in content. Students crowded to his lectures, some from other faculties. As all the seats in the lecture room were taken, students sat on the floor or on the steps of the lecture rostrum. At that time the two Christian groups that made most impact on the university students were CICCU and the Franciscans, who centred on St. Benet's Church. The CICCU had a strong Evangelical tradition; the Franciscans a firm Catholic tradition. There was very little communication between the two groups. During a lecture on the Atonement, Professor Ramsey urged all who belonged to either tradition to begin communicating. "You are much closer to each other than you imagine," he said. "In your different ways you are both trying to preserve the heart of the Gospel. What we need is an outpouring of the Holy Spirit to help you communicate and understand each other."

The summer of 1952 saw the completion of my time at university. Many of my contemporaries went to serve abroad. I did not go overseas myself as originally planned. I was advised by my medical specialist that this would be most unwise with my physical disability. Instead, with my degree in Theology, I was able to take up a post in charge of Scripture at St. Albans Grammar School for Girls. I served there for nine extraordinarily happy and fulfilling years. The Headmistress, Miss Gladys Dwyer, was very progressive. To a school that steadily increased to about eight hundred and fifty girls, she appointed a number of enthusiastic and energetic staff. She gave much encouragement to every department. The Scripture department grew. At one time there were approximately two dozen girls taking A Level Scripture, with some going on to university to study Theology.

By 1957, I was the deputy headmistress. This was not a position I had sought. It seemed right to accept Miss Dwyer's invitation, especially as it would sometimes involve being responsible for school assemblies. By 1960, Miss Dwyer was urging me to apply for headships. Again, I had no ambitions in this direction. She was so insistent that I felt I must investigate this possibility.

Outside school, I had no personal responsibilities. My parents were fit and very active in pursuing their own interests. I was free to go anywhere in the country. After much thought and prayer, I resolved to apply for every headship advertised in the Times Educational Supplement, for which I had the minimum qualifications. I would trust the Lord to lead me to the post of His choice.

In November, I was invited to attend two interviews, one in Birkenhead and one in Bexhill. I travelled to Birkenhead where it was foggy and so icy on the pavements that it was difficult to keep standing. To my great relief, I was not offered the post. I journeyed straight from Birkenhead to Bexhill for a first round of interviews. I was delighted subsequently to be offered the headship at Bexhill Grammar School for Girls. As I returned by train back to St. Albans, the winter sun was shining over the sea and Cooden Beach. I was very thankful to God that He had called me to Bexhill and not to Birkenhead! In April 1961, I took up my new post at the Grammar School.

I inherited a loyal and very competent staff. Every head of department was enthusiastic about her subject, jostling for space on the school timetable and for financial resources. Academic results were good. Music, art, drama and physical education were all of a high standard and enriched the life of the school. Daily school assemblies gave a strong sense of community and belonging.

The head of the Scripture department, like her colleagues, was keen to promote her subject. In 1962 I supported her in arranging our first annual conference on Christian discipleship at Ashburnham. As Michael Townroe and Edmund Heddle were two of our school governors, we invited them to be our first speakers.

In 1965 the new head of Scripture was eager to continue the tradition and took a prominent part in organising the weekend in which we experienced so much blessing. For several years following, weekends at Ashburnham played a significant role in senior girls coming to a genuine Christian faith.

Throughout 1967 the sense of call to a wider ministry, which I had begun to experience in the previous year, deepened. 1967 and 1968 were years filled with many initiatives of the Holy Spirit in blessing people's lives. I would include myself in their number. Yet I was very aware that I was still standing behind God's tapestry and there were many loose ends. The complete healing from my physical disability made new horizons possible. Throughout 1967 two questions were uppermost in my mind. One was the possibility of marriage, the other the possibility of Christian service overseas.'

In 1967 I had a developing relationship with a gifted and sensitive Christian man, filled with the Holy Spirit and uncompromising in his zeal for the Lord. We were occupied together in a number of evangelistic and pastoral enterprises. I assisted with a holiday club for children and young people. In the previous year we had arranged outings to hear Billy Graham. Will and Vi Sidnell, frequently invited my friend to have supper with us on Sunday evenings. These were times of good fellowship and growth in spiritual understanding of many things. He had a firm call to serve the Lord overseas. As the weeks passed, it became clear that my deepening feelings were not reciprocated.

I still felt the need to explore opportunities for service overseas although I must say I was filled with apprehension at the prospect. I approached two missionary societies and in both cases, there were no suitable openings. For some months my doctor friend, Marguerite von Bergen, had been urging me to visit her in Burundi for the summer holidays and for a tour into Rwanda and Southern Uganda. She wanted to assist me in my efforts to discover whether I should be serving overseas.

In July 1967 I set off for Burundi. I spent three weeks with Marguerite at Ibuye, meeting and worshipping with Africans who had a lively faith. I visited the hospital where the love of Jesus was very evident in all the Christian staff and helpers. Marguerite seemed to have so much responsibility. She was responsible for everything, including the surgery. She had four weeks' leave due, so we travelled North into Rwanda. We spent two days in a refugee settlement and two days at Gahini, a most idyllic and beautiful spot. We then made our way into Uganda, spending a few days at the leper colony in the middle of Lake Bunyoni. We journeyed on to Kampala, staying two days en route in the Queen Elizabeth game park.

Our venue in Kampala was the Church Missionary Society guest house, close to the Anglican cathedral. Marguerite had arranged some helpful visits. One afternoon we went to the leading girls' school in Uganda, Gayaza High School, for tea with the headmistress. It was quite clear that my particular qualifications would not be useful in their educational world. If I could have offered mathematics or sciences there would have been some openings. In schools and training colleges Africans were replacing Europeans as heads and principals, whenever possible. A visit to Mukono Theological College also had a negative result. The only opportunity for women was in the training of prospective pastors' wives to run their households well. Hardly my scene!

It seemed the Holy Spirit was saying, "No!" to service overseas. This was confirmed in a most extraordinary and unexpected way. Dr. Helen Roseveare had been a member of the CWICCU in my Homerton days. I discovered she was staying for awhile just round the corner from the CMS guest house. She was waiting to return to the Congo. During a time of furlough in the United Kingdom, she had concluded that England was in greater need of missionaries than Africa. I explained my situation. In response she advised, "Do not go abroad unless the path is very, very clear!" These words seemed to contain God's now word for me. I returned home at the beginning of September confident that the Lord's plan for me was to remain in England and Bexhill.

Towards the end of the month I received a letter from John Bickersteth to his prayer partners. His letter was inspired by a vision of Mr. Kenneth Gibson, a recently retired business man and deeply committed Christian from Hailsham.

John described a proposed nine-month Bible research course. Those who took part, would meet once a month on a Saturday for the whole day. The intention was that each Bible researcher should spend the previous month in intensive study, attempting to find the answer to a challenging question. They would also, with the help of God's Spirit, seek to put into practise all they were learning. No reference books were to be used; only the Bible and a concordance were permitted. The Holy Spirit alone was to be the Teacher. The questions were very relevant for everyday Christian living and included such topics as:

How can I pray effectively?

How can I be filled with God's love?

How can I have the faith that moves mountains?

I could see that this was a course that could transform a Christian's life so I went to the first meeting. By the end of the day, I was convinced that taking this course was the next step for discovering God's will.

In the following months, the five researchers who completed the course grew close in fellowship. Our studies proved to be life-changing and dynamic. One month when we were studying how the promises of God could be claimed, three of us were led to the same passages from the Book of Isaiah. These included the promise from Chapter 44 that God was going to pour out His Spirit on His people. In the light of all that had been happening in the area, the five of us had the same impression. We felt that God was preparing us for Revival in East Sussex. We knelt to pray to commit ourselves to this vision. John led us in prayer. He asked God to use us, five weak people, as Jesus used the five loaves, in any way He chose to feed the multitudes of East Sussex. Early in the new year of 1968, John opened Ashburnham Place once a month on a Monday evening. He invited anyone who wished to join him in prayer for East Sussex. Three dozen or so people from different Church traditions responded to this invitation.

In June 1968 I attended an ordination service at which Edmund Heddle preached on the verse: "Not by might, nor by power, but by My Spirit says the Lord of Hosts." Zechariah 4:6. These words spoke to me. It seemed that God was saying that although secular position and professional expertise could be used by Him, nothing of lasting spiritual value could be achieved without the blessing and power of the Holy Spirit. In July I made an appointment to see Mr. Rendell Jones, the Chief Education Officer, before the school summer holidays.

The Boys' Grammar School and the Girls' School were on the same site next door to each other. The local Education Authority planned to amalgamate the two schools, when the headmaster retired in 1972. I felt an urgency to tell Mr. Jones that when the amalgamation took place I would not be applying for the headship. I wanted him to know that I believed I had wider Christian work to do in East Sussex. He was not altogether surprised as I had helped him with training weekends for primary and secondary school Scripture teachers. He said that the Education Committee had been thinking of appointing a Religious Education Adviser for the county, when there were sufficient funds. He suggested this might be a suitable post for me when the time came to leave the Grammar School. This was a useful proposition for us both to leave on the table.

During the summer holidays, however, the headmaster of the Boys' School died suddenly of a heart attack. Mr. Jones 'phoned me at the beginning of the autumn term to say the amalgamation would now take place in a year's time. He asked whether I felt the same as in July about the future. I answered, "Yes".

There were two more incidents in the autumn of 1968, which helped to point the way ahead. The first was a visit to the school one Friday afternoon of John Bickersteth. He had come to speak to members of the Christian Union. It was my practice to entertain speakers in my room to tea, before they went to talk to the girls. While we were having tea, John suddenly asked, "Miss Wheeler, what is preventing you from devoting yourself to prayer and the ministry of the Word?" Acts 6:4. He had come with a message from Mrs. Eva Lowe, who had three daughters at the Grammar School. Eva had been involved in the Monday evening meetings for prayer for East Sussex. For some months John had been encouraging her in an intercessory ministry. During a time of prayer, she had been given some scriptures for me from St. Paul's second letter to the Corinthians:-

> "It is God Who establishes us with you in Christ and has commissioned us.
> He has put this seal upon us and given His Spirit in our hearts as a guarantee." 2Corinthians 1:21-22.
> "Not that we are sufficient of ourselves to claim anything as coming from us; our sufficiency is from God, Who has qualified us to be ministers of a new covenant, not in a written code but in the Spirit; for the written code kills but the Spirit gives life." 2Corinthians 3:5-6.

Eva thought God was calling me to leave the Grammar School and to go out into East Sussex to share the Good News.

The next day another insight pointed in the same direction. During the autumn two new Bible research courses had begun, led by four of the original researchers. I helped to lead a Saturday group with Kenneth Gibson. During a time of sharing, a group member, Mr. Terrell Boyes, made a challenging contribution. He had come to the conclusion that I should be leaving the Grammar School to engage in an itinerate ministry in East Sussex. The purpose would be to encourage people to prepare for Revival, through prayer and study of the scriptures.

I questioned Terrell closely. The next afternoon, I called to see Eva. In those days I still called her "Mrs. Lowe". I needed to ask her a number of questions. After leaving her, I attended church where we sang the well-known hymn:
> Jesus calls us o'er the tumult
> Of our life's wild restless sea,"

The second verse had a particularly potent effect:
> "As of old apostles heard it
> By the Galilean lake.
> Turned from home, and toil, and kindred,
> Leaving all for His dear sake."

It was the word 'toil' that was so poignant. It seemed I had to give up my actual toil and work at school. I can remember feeling quite elated that I would not have to make any more school timetables!

I knew I must take Eva's and Terrell's insights seriously. The next step would be for the call to be tested by other members of the Body of Christ.

Chapter Four

Testing the Call

"Do not quench the Spirit…..but test everything". 1Thessalonians 5:19-20

I was now to experience something of God's wonderful provision. As I prepared to leave the Grammar School, the truth of Jesus' words, that our Heavenly Father cares about our everyday needs, was marvellously proved: "Seek first His Kingdom and His righteousness and all these things shall be yours as well." Matthew 6:33.

Three of my Christian brothers set about testing my call to go out into East Sussex - John Bickersteth, Edmund Heddle and Kenneth Gibson. They were cautious about me giving up my post at the Grammar School. Edmund, in particular as my minister, felt the weight of responsibility. They seemed to be in somewhat of a dilemma, sensing on one hand that God was calling me into a new work, and yet very concerned about my future security.

They decided to pray for a financial 'Gideon' sign. They agreed between themselves sums of money that should be available, before commissioning me to work in East Sussex. Months later they told me that they covenanted to keep the amounts secret between themselves. They prayed for £2,000 for three consecutive years a lot of money in those days! No emotional appeals for money or support were made. A simple statement was given by John at one of the monthly Ashburnham, East Sussex prayer meetings. He said, "We have been praying now for over a year for Revival in East Sussex. It seems that God may be calling full-time workers into ministry to help prepare people for God's coming amongst us. It looks as though Miss Wheeler will be the first. If you feel you should do anything practical about this, please get in touch with me."

Meanwhile I thought it important to begin making my own preparations. I planned to leave school at the end of the summer term. To do this I would need to give notice immediately after the Easter holidays. I therefore arranged to spend a week at the Crowhurst Home of Healing, right away from everyone I knew, to listen to God for myself.

I became convinced that if I was to receive an answer to my questionings, I should begin taking practical steps that would help me to be ready to answer the call. I had recently heard an address based on Hebrews chapter

11, about the Old Testament saints, who had acted in faith in response to God's call. A striking interpretation was given of the introductory words: "faith is the substance of things hoped for, the evidence of things not seen". This means, said the speaker, "treating the future which God has promised as real". He continued something like this, "Noah built an ark for protection from the flood, before there was any rain in sight. Abraham had to do the modern equivalent of putting his house on the market and buy tents and animals in preparation for a nomadic life". It became clear to me that if I was going to travel round East Sussex, I would need a new and reliable car. My knowledge of mechanics was very limited! My current car had been in an accident and needed replacing.

At this point I embarked on my first small step of financial faith. I consulted the garage owners who looked after my car. They recommended a particular model that would be suitable for my purposes and offered a price for my old car. I then calculated the financial commitments I would need to meet in the month ahead, before I received my next salary cheque. These included everything required for housekeeping, as I did not feel it right to expose my friends, Will and Vi Sidnell to any anxiety in this matter. I would also need to pay the mortgage and the rates. I found I had just sufficient in the bank to buy the car and to meet these obligations. There would, however, be nothing left to purchase a much-needed pair of summer shoes, for the beginning of the summer term. My old summer shoes were very shabby indeed. As a Christian woman I had always considered it important to look my best. Wearing old-fashioned styles and worn out clothes in a community of girls and young women would not be a good testimony. The platform in the school hall was high and the feet of the headmistress very much in view during school assemblies! I decided the new shoes were very desirable but not essential and so resolved to trust the Lord in this small matter. I purchased the new car before going to Crowhurst.

On 8th April 1969 I arrived at the Home of Healing. I was expectant and as open as I was capable of being to the leading of God, but with a natural fear of what the future might hold. I had an overwhelming anxiety that if I followed the Lord's path without reserve, I might end up in prison or solitary confinement. The source of this apprehension probably came from the stories of Christians I had met or read about, who endured such sufferings during the war years. From the moment I arrived, there was a tremendous sense of the Lord's presence. He spoke into my mind words of great encouragement:

> "I have brought you here so that you will learn to rest in Me and to show you how to receive My gift of faith. I want you to know and feel My love as you have never felt it before, so that you will not be afraid. My perfect love casts out fear".

Early in my visit, I was sitting in the garden enjoying sunshine and conversation with one of the other guests. She had visited Crowhurst on previous occasions and mentioned how in the past, she had found the ministry there so helpful. I asked her to explain. She then shared how she had found the ministries of laying-on-of-hands and anointing with oil very strengthening and healing. During her first visit, through laying-on-of-hands, she had received healing from a nervous breakdown. After two years, she returned to test a calling to minister to those suffering from breakdowns and to seek complete healing for service. She then shared how the anointing had been a much deeper experience than that of the laying-on-of-hands. I found myself identifying with her. I too was at Crowhurst to test a calling. I also needed further healing. Although I had received a wonderful healing when I was baptised in the Spirit, I still experienced irrational fears. I asked myself: "Was the next step forward to be anointed?"

Guests at Crowhurst are encouraged to relax. Breakfast is brought to their rooms so that they can be relieved from the burden of socialising early in the day. Over breakfast I was reading one of a number of books which had been placed in my room, 'Christ Healing' by the Reverend Howard Cobb, the founder of the healing ministry at Crowhurst. Well into his book, he describes the difference between laying-on-of-hands and anointing with oil. I could not ignore the fact that twice within twenty-four hours the Holy Spirit had drawn my attention to the significance of anointing. Immediately, some words from Psalm 23 came into my mind: "Thou anointest my head with oil, my cup overflows". I asked the Lord if there was any further passages of Scripture I should look at for light and guidance. Straightaway I thought of the account of the anointing of King Saul, the first King of Israel. I looked up the story in the first Book of Samuel Chapter 10. It was amazing how relevant the circumstances were to my own.

While Saul was away from home looking for his father's lost asses, he met the prophet Samuel, who anointed him as future king. Samuel then told him that on the way home he would be given three signs from God, confirming his call to be King. First he would meet two men who would say to him, "The asses which you went to seek are found, and now your father has ceased to care about the asses and is anxious about you." Secondly, Saul would meet three men of God going to Bethel to worship. They would greet Saul and give him two loaves of bread which he was to accept. Saul's third meeting would be with a band of prophets, making music and prophesying, returning from a place of worship. At that point the Spirit of the Lord would come mightily upon him and he would prophesy with the prophets and be turned into another man.

These three signs, given to Saul, had extraordinary parallels to my own situation. Firstly my father was exceedingly anxious about me giving up my post at the Bexhill Grammar School. He had made such remarks as, "You are more extreme than John Wesley! I don't know any minister who has ever done such a thing!" It was of course very natural for a father to be concerned about the future security of his daughter. Through the story of Saul, it seemed that God was saying, "Your father is going to stop worrying about your means of livelihood. He will be more concerned about what is really best for you and the fulfilment of My calling."

Secondly, I was still waiting to hear the results of the prayers of my three men of God. The three men, travelling to Bethel to worship, gave Saul provision and sustenance. It seemed as though the Spirit was pointing out to me that whatever the Lord's three servants offered, I should accept.

Thirdly, I had been concerned that the new calling would be lonely and isolated. The Lord seemed to be assuring me, through the story of the band of prophets, that there would be a significant number of people involved with me in His work. There would be a working together with others who were filled with the Holy Spirit.

I concluded that God was clearly calling me to be anointed. This should take place while I was still at Crowhurst as a step of faith and for my strengthening and equipping for future ministry. I consulted the Reverend Harry Weston who was in pastoral charge at Crowhurst, during an interregnum. The Spirit witnessed to him that God had been speaking and he agreed to anoint me and to pray for my enabling for the future.

Before the anointing I wrote to Mr. Jones to ask to see him about handing in my resignation for the end of the summer term. I also wrote to Michael Townroe as Chairman of Governors, sharing with him how God had been leading.

I was anointed in the Old Chapel and signed with the sign of the Cross. It was a most reassuring experience, with a deep awareness of the Lord's healing presence. Prayers were offered that my fears would be taken away, that no powers of the Evil One would harm me and that I would know great freedom in the Spirit. The first thing I noticed as I looked up, was the picture by Herbert Beecroft of the Lord turning and looking at Peter. It seemed that the eyes of the Lord were looking directly into mine and that He spoke these words from St. John's Gospel: "You have not chosen Me but I have chosen you and ordained you that you should bring forth much fruit and that your fruit should remain".

While I was away at Crowhurst, Eva Lowe had been praying for me. She had been reading some Scripture Union Bible notes, which included the story of the anointing of King Saul! Without knowing what had happened, she had become convinced that I should be anointed. This was a marvellous confirmation of the rightness of all that had taken place.

When I returned to Bexhill, the three signs were fulfilled within a few days. The first, while my parents were staying with me for the last part of the Easter holidays. My father was much more relaxed and accepting about the new calling and did not oppose my recent commitment. The Lord gave me a lovely bonus through my parents, in addition to my father's approval! My mother, unwittingly, was used to give a very special sign of His intention to provide everything necessary, to the smallest detail. Before returning home, she asked me, "Would you mind if I gave you your birthday present a month early? I would like to go with you to buy a new pair of shoes!" She actually bought me two pairs! Our God is indeed a great God Who does "exceedingly abundantly above all that we could ask or think" in both small and great matters.

A few days later John Bickersteth 'phoned me with the news of the fulfilment of the second sign. He was very awed indeed by what had happened. The requests of the three men, for my provision, had been more than granted. For years two and three of my anticipated East Sussex journeyings £2,000 to the exact penny had been promised for each year. For the first year exactly £3,000 had been donated. John went on to comment, "There must be some need that will arise in the first year, that we haven't thought about".

John then continued, "An amazing variety of gifts have been promised, some large and some small. Together they have added up to exactly what was requested, plus an additional £1,000". To me this was the beginning of the fulfilment of the third sign. There must be numbers of people standing with me, open to the guiding of the Holy Spirit. Each provider must have listened very carefully to God. It was clear that the Lord was gathering those who were willing to move forward together with Him to fulfil His purposes.

When I shared all my news with Michael Townroe he responded, "Laus Deo!" meaning "Praise God!" There would be numerous occasions in the future when he would use these words.

I found it both awe-inspiring and reassuring that so many Christian friends had been involved in testing my East Sussex calling.

Grammar School Farewell Celebrations

With some of the junior girls – Michael Townroe looking on in the background.
Photo: Bexhill Observer

With some of the prefects.
Photo: Bexhill Observer

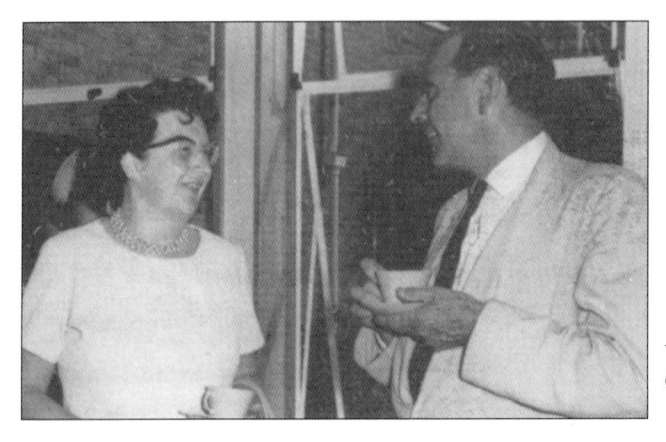

With Chief Education Officer, Mr Rendell Jones.
Photo: Bexhill Observer

Chapter Five
Commissioned to Serve in East Sussex

"After fasting and praying they laid theirs hands on them and sent them off". Acts 13:3

"Do not fear what men say but speak My Word boldly. Though all hell oppose you, I stand with you, your God, your Rock and your Deliverer".

This was the message given as the Elders of Beulah Baptist Church laid hands on me and sent me out into East Sussex. The words were challenging, anticipating spiritual warfare and conflict ahead. They were most appropriate as we were meeting on the Feast of St. Michael and all Angels. My parents and two hundred or so Christian friends from differing Church traditions had gathered to acknowledge my calling, to pray and send me on my way.

Edmund Heddle presided at the service, Michael Townroe led intercessions and John Bickersteth preached.

After the laying-on-of-hands by Beulah Elders, Michael and John gave me the right hand of fellowship. They expressed their conviction that it was God Who had called me into ministry. Michael used these words of blessing: "The Lord bless your going out and your coming in from this time forth for evermore". John gave these words of affirmation and exhortation: "We recognise your call to be of God and we offer you the right hand of fellowship in His Name. Trust in the Lord with all your heart and lean not to your own insight, in all your ways acknowledge Him and He will direct your path".

Michael then offered prayers for the Church and people of East Sussex:
"Almighty God, who hast promised to hear the prayers of those who ask in faith:
- grant that there may be in our midst that quickening and revival which flows from a renewal of our love and obedience;
- give Thy blessing to Thy servant Eileen Wheeler as she responds to Thy call to serve without condition or reserve;
- help us to gain a new vision of Thy purpose and a new zeal in Thy service.......

We pray to Thee in particular for all who live around us, especially in this area of East Sussex:
- grant that we may be found faithful in our witness, through word and deed;
- grant to all in positions of leadership and trust a sense of responsibility and a readiness to know and do Thy will;

- inspire all clergy and ministers, teachers and writers and all who in particular ways, influence the lives of others that they may lead always in the ways of righteousness and truth".

After these prayers, John preached. He reminded us of the story of Joshua when he had just crossed the River Jordan into the Promised Land. He was waiting before Jericho, when a man appeared before him with a drawn sword in his hand. Joshua asked: "Are you for us or for our adversaries?" The man replied: "As Commander of the army of the Lord I have now come". Joshua realised he was in the presence of the Lord and fell down on his face to the earth in worship.

John continued by likening our situation to that of Joshua and the children of Israel. We were just inside the Promised Land of the Holy Spirit, waiting to take up our full inheritance. "We are called to be with Jesus, as Commander of the armies of the Lord. He has drawn His sword. He has taken over this Revival. The Kingdom is His and He will not give His glory to another".

After his address, John invited members of the congregation, who wished to serve the Lord uncompromisingly in East Sussex, to stand for prayer. Thirty to forty people stood. One was Eva Lowe, who had already been praying for me and knew that God was calling her to continue this intercessory ministry on my behalf. It was very encouraging to know that significant numbers of the Lord's people were responding to His call to work together for the fulfilment of His purposes.

The next day I set out with some words of Edmund still ringing in my ears. The truth they contained would be the basis of all that I would do in the future: "All true ministry is based upon the Word and the Spirit. Not the Word without the Spirit, which leads to barren dogmatism. Not upon the Spirit without the Word, which leads to fanaticism but upon the Word by the Spirit. I believe that God has yet much light and truth to break forth from His Word. Eileen, this is your commission. You can only bring this forth by the Holy Spirit and He will enable you to do it in accordance with God's revealed truth".

With John Bickersteth and the Beulah elders, Edmund Heddle, Jim Twaddle and Will Sidwell, after the commissioning to serve in East Sussex.

Photo: Bexhill Observer

Chapter Six

Out and About in East Sussex

"Every place that the sole of your foot will tread upon I have given you." Joshua 1:3

Three months into my East Sussex journeyings I knew why the extra £1,000 had been given for the first year's ministry. My friends, Will and Vi Sidnell, were seriously ill over Christmas with influenza. Their sons were keen for them to return to St. Albans.

I needed to find £2,000 for their share in the house. Miraculously, the provision for this was already available. There was the £1,000 gift. Also, convinced that I would never return to the teaching profession, I had previously estimated that about £1,000 superannuation was due to me. We were therefore in a position to start making plans for Will and Vi to move during the summer months.

Against this background of planning for a major change in life-style, there were numerous openings for ministry. There were requests for Bible research courses from adult and young people. In the New Year, groups emerged in Barcombe, Ashburnham and Hailsham. These included a group for clergy wives and another group for ministers' wives. Other groups were to follow in Battle, Bexhill, Herstmonceux, St. Leonards, Berwick and Seaford. There were invitations to speak in Hastings and St. Leonards, in Battle, Sedlescombe, Wadhurst, Jarvis Brook and East Grinstead. It was most inspiring to find people from all kinds of social backgrounds, from different Christian traditions, both young and old, seeking earnestly to know the Lord. It was exciting that so many were seeing their prayers answered. Significant numbers were being released and baptised in the Spirit and coming to know God in new ways. Everyone's experience was unique and special. The Holy Spirit was meeting each individual at their particular point of need. Enquiries from young men and women were numerous. To meet their need, with Eva Lowe's help, I arranged two Saturdays of prayer and ministry.

During the early months of 1970, there were two important days of praise and prayer for women in East Sussex. These were exceptional occasions held in the Great Hall of Ashburnham Place and were to have far-reaching consequences. Both events were held in response to revelation given to Eva, as she continued to pray for me and my East Sussex travels. One day I called to see her on my way home. She was ironing in the kitchen. Lying on the ironing board was a rough sketch she had made of the outside of a large Georgian-looking house. "Where is this house you have visited?" she asked. "I have seen you speaking there in a large room to numbers of women who were being greatly blessed". To my knowledge I had not been inside such a house.

A few days later I was visiting another friend. She had a postcard of Ashburnham Place on her mantelpiece. The picture focused on the central part of the house, which was reflected in the front lake. The side wings of the building seemed hardly noticeable. "That is the house Eva drew!" I thought. "We are to hold a day of praise and prayer for women in the Great Hall at Ashburnham."

When I showed Eva the postcard she recognised the house in her vision. Shortly afterwards I was reading from the Revised Version of the Psalms. My attention was drawn to the translation of Psalm 68:11: "The Lord giveth the word. The women that publish the tidings are a great host". It seemed to me that the Lord was planning to do a special work in East Sussex through Christian women. This was so clear that we booked the Great Hall for a day in January.

On the day we were to meet, there was a sprinkling of snow on the ground, with the promise of more to come. Many had been suffering from influenza over Christmas and the New Year. Humanly speaking, there was much to discourage people from making the journey to Ashburnham. However, a company of about seventy women gathered. They came in twos and threes from an area extending as far as Ditchling to the west, Rye to the east and inland to East Grinstead. We began with a short time of worship and prayer based on Psalm 68. The rest of the morning was spent in giving testimony to the new things God was doing amongst us; in our varied situations and circumstances; in our families and in our churches. The Spirit gave a glorious freedom in sharing. Naturally reserved women were not afraid to speak out. The afternoon was spent in praise and prayer for East Sussex. There was a tremendous sense that a work of Revival was beginning and a great eagerness to meet again soon.

As Eva and I thought and prayed about the future, the plans for another day of praise and prayer in May began to unfold. One day she said to me, "I think the next day of prayer should be based on the passage from St. John's Gospel about the Vine and the branches and should finish with a Communion service with you presiding." Such a suggestion was totally unexpected and would need to be weighed and tested very carefully. Eva was absolutely certain that this was what the Lord had shown her. Nothing would shake her. As a member of a Baptist church, I would, in theory, be able to do this because of the strong emphasis in that tradition on the priesthood of all believers. However, at least half of the women with whom we were in touch came from traditions that would have reservations about a woman presiding at Communion. There was much to be considered as I knew Eva's vision for the day would be controversial.

I firmly believed that in all ministry and outreach, it was important and Biblical for me to remain under' the authority of those who had commissioned me to serve in East Sussex. It was therefore crucial that I consulted my 'three wise men' as Eva and I had affectionately come to think of Michael, John and Edmund. They had each taken a pastoral responsibility for my general well-being. Every week I met with one of them to give an account of my stewardship and to receive their advice and encouragement. I prayed and waited to be shown what I should share with them.

Edmund gave his cautious blessing to proceed on condition that it was a one-off occasion. He had difficulties because of the Baptist emphasis on the Gathered Church. Historically, it has been the custom in this tradition to meet at the Lord's Table with those who have covenanted to meet together regularly in the same local congregation. Edmund was very concerned that I should not be seen to be starting a new church!

One evening Michael and his wife Beatrice came to coffee at my home in Chantry Avenue. I had received a gift of a praise plaque from the Mary Sisters in Darmstadt. Michael coveted the plaque for the St. Peter's churchyard and he and Beatrice had come to discuss this possibility.

As we talked Michael changed the subject, asking, "Are you going to have another day of praise and prayer?" "Yes" I said, "but I am not quite sure how I should proceed. Eva thinks we should finish the day with a Communion service. How do you feel about this?" "I think it would be a very good thing if you had an Agape" he replied. "This is often done on the Continent between Roman Catholics and Protestants, with a simple service and fellowship meal of sharing bread together." "The difficulty with that" I said, "is that the main Scripture passage for the day is to be about the Vine and the branches. This would seem to suggest that we should be using wine during the service. I have not yet decided what we should do. Please could you pray that I will make the right decision."

Beatrice had been at our first day of praise and prayer. She was a very positive and prayerful support in so much that I was seeking to do. As Michael was the Rural Dean at the time, I did not want to put her in the embarrassing situation of feeling she had to leave us halfway through the day. By the time I sent out the invitations, I had decided to go ahead with a simple Communion service within a Baptist-Congregational framework and I wrote a note to this effect on Beatrice's invitation. I was delighted that she joined us and took part fully in our day of prayer, praise and celebration.

I needed to know how much to share with John. We would be meeting in his home and I expected that his wife, Marlis, would be with us again. I anticipated that should he give his full blessing to our plans and he received any complaints from ministers or clergy in the area, he could be in trouble with his Bishop. I therefore went to my regular meeting with John, asking the Lord to show me exactly what to do and say. As soon as I arrived John said, "I have a message from Marlis. She is very sorry that she won't be able to be with you on your next day of prayer and praise. We both have to be away for the whole day at Richard's prep school." This seemed to give very clear guidance not to tell John the details of our programme. If there should be any subsequent difficulties or complaints, he could not in any way be held responsible.

On a lovely day in May, approximately one hundred and twenty women gathered at Ashburnham. Most of them did not know the plan to share Communion together during the afternoon. We spent a most wonderful time together in the presence of the Lord. The chairs were set out in several large oval-shaped arrangements, facing each other. The day began with worship and hymns of praise, followed by a time of testimony from women all round the room. They had much to share of God's great blessings since we had last met, including a testimony of healing. There was an orderly freedom in the Spirit to speak and a strong sense that everyone was of 'one accord'.

After a coffee break, we studied the beginning of Chapter 15 of St. John's Gospel with its allegory of Jesus, the true Vine and we as the branches. We saw the great importance of being totally one with Him and with one another. We could see that for Revival and new spiritual life to come to the area, we, the Lord's people, must be seen to be in love with Him and each other, prepared to lay down our lives for our friends. We all needed to draw from the life of Jesus Himself. As He filled us with His Spirit, we would be able to love and obey Him and serve one another. In this way, we would be able to live very fruitful lives to the glory of God the Father.

At the end of the morning, we sat in silence together. Each one was to decide between themselves and the Lord whether they should take part in the Communion service. Sharing the Bread and Wine together would be a token of our desire to be totally at one with the Lord and one another. Every person present decided this was what they should do. The presence of the

Spirit and the unity expressed were truly amazing, felt and tangible. After we had all received the Bread and Wine, there was a deep silence, broken by someone reverently saying: "Praise the Lord!" I think those words summed up everyone's feelings. We had been on holy ground.

Somehow that day dispersed clouds of oppression and spiritual darkness in peoples' spirits. During the following weeks, numbers of those present began to receive new hymns and songs of praise and devotion. It seemed the Lord was showing us that our coming-together had given Him much pleasure. Most of the women concerned had no musical expertise. Some of the songs were given during prayer times but often while ordinary everyday tasks were being done. Beautiful words and tunes were given while the washing was being hung out or the breakfast things being washed up. One lady was singing a new song when her husband returned from the kitchen with an early morning cup of tea! The Lord was pouring out a Spirit of praise to equip us to fight future spiritual battles.

For me, the weeks following our very special day were spent preparing for Will and Vi Sidnell to leave for St. Albans. They left during the third week of July. This was a great upheaval for me and a time of readjustment. We had lived together for seventeen years and their departure seemed like a bereavement. For some time the sense of desolation was very real and at times, overwhelming. The Lord was very gracious and gave me many encouragements. I knew He was with me, caring for me and guiding me. He showed me that without delay, I was to get the house ready to receive guests; some would come as house guests, others in groups for study, fellowship and prayer.

Will and Vi had taken their furniture with them. I set about making a list of all the basic things needed to make the home comfortable for visitors. I had £300 to spend as the cheque I received from my superannuation was £1,300. This was more than I had expected. When I had purchased everything I needed except an electric fire for the main sitting room, I had only £10 left. I needed a large and efficient fire to replace the coal fire that Will and Vi had enjoyed. I thought I should wait until I could afford to buy something suitable.

The same day that I made this decision I was working in the front garden, when a neighbour stopped and asked, "How are you getting on?" "Very well" I replied, "I have finished rearranging the rooms and furniture. The only thing I have to buy now is an electric fire for the sitting room." The gentleman then said, "I hope you won't be offended by my suggestion. We have just bought a new electric fire. We cannot use it because the base is too wide for our fireplace. Would you like to buy it for £10?"

I went to look at the fire. It was tastefully coloured with alternating dark and light grey areas, edged with gold. These colourings were exactly the same as the tiles surrounding my own fireplace. This was such a special sign to me of the Lord's love and care and of His intention to lead and provide. It was a reminder too of Jesus' promise that, if we make seeking God's Kingdom a priority, our everyday needs will be met. There was no need to be anxious about the future!

Chapter Seven

Surprises!

"'My thoughts are not your thoughts, neither are your ways My ways', says the Lord." Isaiah 55:8

"If you had lived in the Middle Ages, you would have been an Abbess!" These were words of Michael Townroe. I had just shared with him and Beatrice, the first songs given to me by the Spirit.

I had been living on my own for several days, when I found myself singing a tune of longing and sadness. I had been reading the story of the crucifixion from St. John's Gospel. The account included Jesus' words, "I thirst" and "It is finished". In the song Jesus Himself seemed to be speaking about the longing of His heart:

> "I AM the Lord Your God,
> I AM the Lord Your God.
> I thirst for souls!
> I thirst for souls!
> My thirst is still unsatisfied.
> I thirst for souls! I thirst for souls!
> My dying love to satisfy.
>
> My work is finished
> My work is finished.
> But few take heed!
> But few take heed!
> My heart is broken and I weep.
> But few take heed!
> But few take heed!
> I long for love from those I freed."

The sense of the Lord's grief was intense. He longed for intimacy with those He had died to forgive. The fact that our love mattered so much to Him, filled me with awe. It seemed important not to lose the words or tune, so I recorded them on to a tape, as I could not write music.

The next day a missionary on furlough arrived to stay with me for several days. She was suffering from deep depression and had been sent to me by her minister. She shared with me about her life in India. As she talked, I became convinced that some influence of darkness and oppression had effected her, possibly as a result of visits to Hindu temples. During the night and early morning, when I was praying for her, I was given another song. This time it was one of praise and victory:

> "Thank You Lord Jesus!
> Thank You Lord Jesus!
> Thank You for Your precious cleansing blood.
> Thank You Lord Jesus!
> Thank You Lord Jesus!
> Thank You for Your precious dying love.
>
> All praise Lord Jesus!
> All praise Lord Jesus!
> All praise to Your glorious mighty Name.
> All praise Lord Jesus!
> All praise Lord Jesus!
> All praise for Your glorious saving reign.
>
> Glory Lord Jesus!
> Glory Lord Jesus!
> Glory for Your gracious Spirit given.
> Glory Lord Jesus!
> Glory Lord Jesus!
> Glory for Your gracious Spirit's power."

I knew this song was for my guest and that if she began singing it for herself in worship, she would be set free. I saw that thanksgiving for the power of the blood of Jesus, for the power of His Name and the power of His Spirit would overcome the darkness in her spirit. I recorded the song and gave her the tape and my tape recorder. I suggested she played the tape and sang along with the music and the words as frequently as possible throughout the day. Within twenty-four hours, the oppression lifted.

Many more songs and verses were to follow. Women, young and old, began to contact me from all over the area to tell me of new songs they had been given. In October, we held another uplifting day of praise and prayer at Ashburnham. We shared our songs with one another and gave testimony about the circumstances which had inspired them. Joyce Prentice from Eastbourne and Ruth Fletcher from St. Leonards were able to write out the music for us, sometimes composing harmonies as they wrote. The tunes were easy enabling everyone to join in with flowing melody and praise. These were thrilling days. The Lord was close to us in our daily lives. We were full of expectancy, wondering what He would do next.

Another unexpected happening took place at the end of August. The monthly prayer meeting for Revival at Ashburnham was in progress. About two dozen of us had been praying together in the Green Room, when Eva had a vision of a rough surfaced wooden cross. Above it was written a semi-circle of words: 'Stat Crux Dum Volvitur Orbis'. She wrote down all she had seen and showed her drawing and words to John Bickersteth. "Is this Latin?" she asked. "Yes" John replied, "very good Latin. It means: 'The Cross stands while the world revolves'". We felt that God was reminding us that the Cross of Jesus must be absolutely central to everything we thought and did. If, in the future, distressing times came, we must remember that the Cross was invincible.

About six weeks later, a lay reader from St. Leonards, who had been present at the prayer gathering, discovered that the Latin words were the motto of the Carthusian monks. This discovery widened our vision and the scope of our praying. The only Carthusian monastery in the United Kingdom was at Cowfold in Sussex, just over the East Sussex border. John started a correspondence with the Father Prior, who promised that he and his monks would join with us in prayer for the whole county. We began to realise that the Lord was encouraging us to break through the barriers which divided Christians of different traditions. This was part of His preparation for Revival.

Eva started to look for the wooden cross she had seen in the vision. She thought that the place where it was would be significant in bringing the Lord's people together in East Sussex. Once a week for several months, she spent a day driving round the county, visiting churches and chapels. Her search was unsuccessful. Eventually she gave up her travels. Those of us though who met monthly at Ashburnham to pray, knew that it was important not to neglect the inner meaning of the vision. We were to continue in prayer and to do all we could to enter into the unity which was Christ's dying gift to the Church.

Throughout the early months of 1971, the Lord continued to pour out His Spirit on His people.

> "I am sitting in the desert,
> On a dry and dusty plain.
> I am thirsting for the Water,
> That I never thirst again."

These are the words of a folk-style prayer song given to a Bexhill sixth former. She was one of a number of young men and women who were greatly blessed one Saturday in January. I had led a day of prayer and teaching about the Holy Spirit in my home. Clare slipped quietly away at the end of the day. Later she went to Galley Hill, our local beauty spot overlooking the sea, taking her guitar. As she began to play, the Lord gave her the new song and poured out His blessings mightily upon her. This was the beginning of an exceedingly fruitful prophetic ministry in worship and song, both in the United Kingdom and South Africa.

The day for young people was the inspiration of Sarah, a young woman from St. Leonards. She had been helping me for several months with secretarial work. She offered her help, believing that the Lord had called her to do this before she went to Bible College in the autumn. Sarah was a wonderful gift from God. She herself had been blessed with a number of new songs. She worked very hard producing song sheets and booklets with words and music for a variety of occasions, including the days of praise and prayer for women.

A number of us began to plan and pray for another day of worship in the Great Hall at Ashburnham. It became clear that the main focus should be prayer for healing and wholeness. Some of the new hymns and songs were Communion hymns. It seemed that the Lord had been preparing us to meet at His Table again. So we arranged to sit for most of the morning in the Lord's presence, using the new words and music to express our worship. We explored the scriptures and a minister's wife gave testimony to blessing and healing.

Before sharing the Bread and Wine, we used two of the new Communion hymns. First we sang a hymn of devotion:

> "Low at His Throne we bow,
> Jesus our King.
> To Him our lives we bring
> An offering.
> Our hearts and souls we give
> That we to Him may live
> All for His praise.

Low at His Cross we bow,
Jesus the Lamb.
He is triumphant now
Over death's sting!
The nails, the pain, the shame
Proclaim His glorious reign;
Hail, wondrous Name!

Up to His Table led,
Jesus our Head.
Here from His Hand to take
His living food;
His Body giv'n for us,
His precious Blood poured forth,
Our sacrifice."

We then joined in a hymn which began with thanksgiving and finished with some words of promise from the Lord:

"Thank You for Your broken Body,
Given for me! Given for me!
O the wonder! All joy surpassing,
To partake, Your face to see.

Thank you for Your poured out Blood,
Shed for me! Shed for me!
O the wonder! For my healing,
To drink deep, Your wounds to feel.

I will never leave, forsake you,
Rest in Me! Rest in Me!
Share My triumph! Know My victories!
I love you. My love I give."

After everyone had received Communion, those who would like prayer for healing were asked to raise a hand. About a dozen hands went up. Two small groups of women were waiting on both sides of the room, to lay hands on those who asked for prayer. We ministered to each person, one at a time, so that everyone in the room could pray together for each need. We spoke out each request for all to hear. All were greatly blessed and two experienced total physical as well as spiritual healing. One was healed of a serious chest condition. The other was a lady in her early fifties, suffering from arthritis. She had been told that she would be in a wheelchair by the end of the year. Her healing was complete and she went on to take up a heavy and responsible housekeeping post. She is still alive today!

Another encouraging event took place on Good Friday. Michael asked Eva and me if we would arrange three hours of activities for children in St. Peter's Community Centre, while the adults were in church. This was quite a challenge, especially as the number of children who would attend was uncertain. Somewhere between fifty and eighty were expected. We invited several young people to help us and decided that the theme should be: 'Jesus, the Good Shepherd, who had laid down His life for the sheep'. We hired a real Eastern shepherd's costume and equipment. We tried to imagine the shepherd's life and his great love and caring for his sheep. We then made banners out of coloured sugar paper. The children wrote out short verses from the Bible about Jesus, the Shepherd, using coloured crayons. At the end of the three-hour church service, the children were waiting outside the south door. They invited the adults to join them in a procession all round the outside of the church, ending up at the Lychgate. There a man was waiting with a wheelbarrow. It contained materials needed to put in place the Praise Plaque from the Mary Sisters which Michael had coveted. We then sang together:

The praise plaque at St. Peter's placed by the children on Good Friday 1971.

> "There is a green hill far away
> Outside a city wall,
> Where the dear Lord was crucified
> Who died to save us all."

By the end of the summer two of the young people who had helped us with the children, went to Darmstadt to be Mary Sisters.

Our greatest surprise was still to come, in the revelation that unfolded for another gathering of East Sussex women in May. Sometime during Lent, Eva and I met to pray. We were shown that our next special day was to take place between Ascension and Pentecost on 12th May. Historically, this was the coronation of King George VI. Our coming-together was to have a coronation theme as we 'crowned Jesus as our Captain in temptation's hour'. We were to learn more about prayer and the disciplined life of following Jesus on the Narrow Way. We were to make Jesus Lord of our lives.

Two days later Eva shared with me more details. She had seen in a vision a rectangular room, with a small platform to one side. Semi-circles of chairs were arranged round the platform in five small blocks. There were words written across each block of chairs. 'Breaking of Bread' was on the central block. To the left and right were the words ' Baptism in the Spirit' and 'Anointing'. On the block to the far left was 'Baptism' and to the right 'Laying-on-of-hands. The day was to be one of consecration and dedication. Some women whom God was calling were to be anointed with oil for specific ministries. Eva had another complimentary vision. This was the inside of a church, with a sanctuary lamp. A cup on the Communion Table and the two central blocks of pews were highlighted. On one of these was written 'Baptism in the Spirit' and on the other Anointing'.

We concluded that in the morning we were to meet mainly for teaching in the rectangular room. In the afternoon we were to move into the Church for a Communion Service. At the end of the service, anointing with oil for ministry with the laying-on-of-hands would take place. In recent months, it had become increasingly evident that ministries such as encouragement, intercession, teaching the Word and praying for the sick were beginning to emerge.

As Eva sketched the inside of the church she had glimpsed, I felt it was St. Peter's, Bexhill. She was not familiar with the church. After spending some time there, she knew that was where we were to be.

I went to share with Michael the visions and all that had been happening. He weighed everything carefully. He was of the opinion that we were being led by the Spirit and he agreed to celebrate Communion for us. He also undertook to anoint individuals for ministries at the end of the service, with the proviso that we had a long lunch break. He considered it important that there should be plenty of time to think and pray before making such a serious commitment. He was concerned that no one should feel pressurised. He therefore offered to preside at a further service of Communion and anointing a few weeks later for anyone who wished to take longer to pray about their calling.

Bearing in mind that half the women present would have no knowledge of the Book of Common Prayer, Michael made some other helpful suggestions. "Why don't you print out the whole service?" he suggested. "You could intersperse the set prayers with some of the new hymns. Instead of the Prayer for the Church Militant, you could have a time of extempore praise and prayer". We decided to follow this plan.

There was still one piece of the jigsaw missing. Where were we to hold the morning meeting? St. Peter's Community Centre was not available. The only room I knew in Bexhill with a platform at the side was the Elizabeth Room at the De La Warr Pavilion. I went to the Booking Office to make enquiries. I explained what we needed. The response was most unexpected. "Madam, the Manor Barn would be much more suitable for your purposes". "What is that?" I asked. I had totally missed in my reading of the local press, that the renovating of the Barn was a part of Bexhill Council's project for the restoration of the whole Manor site and gardens. "As a matter of fact" the council officer continued, "if you book the Barn for 12th May, you will probably be the first people to use it. The Mayor is opening it on the previous Sunday".

He showed me the architect's plan. The main room was set out exactly as Eva had seen in her vision! I booked the Barn immediately. The Lord had chosen for us a very beautiful spot. It was also so wonderfully convenient. We could spend the quiet time in the lunch hour enjoying the gardens. The walk to St. Peter's in the afternoon would take barely five minutes across the De La Warr Road.

At the end of April, we were given a 'Crowning' hymn to celebrate our special day of proclaiming the Lordship of Christ. Eva was given the words and I was given the tune with simple harmonies:

> "Crown Him! Crown Him! Crown Him!
> Crown with us the God of Love!
> Love Him! Love Him! Love Him!
> Love with us the Holy Dove!

See Him! See Him! See Him!
See with us the Risen Lord!
Know Him! Know Him! Know Him!
Read with us His Holy Word!

Feel Him! Feel Him! Feel Him!
Feel with us His Presence strong!
Hail Him! Hail Him! Hail Him!
Hail with us! To Him belong!

Serve Him! Serve Him! Serve Him!
Serve with us our Lord and King!
Greet Him! Greet Him! Greet Him!
Greet with us our Saviour King!"

We met on a bright sunny day. The Barn was filled with exotic flowers, which had been arranged for the opening the previous Sunday. The details for the whole day were perfect. The oneness in the Spirit at Communion was very real and filled with the loving presence of the Lord. Michael anointed seven women at the end of the service. Three of us who had been previously anointed for ministries, joined him in the laying-on-of-hands. Within a few weeks, five more women were anointed for various ministries at a Communion service celebrated by Michael.

The 'Crowning Day' as we came to call it, had been truly glorious. The next day I heard some wonderful news. An elderly lady, crippled with arthritis, had been at the Communion Service. Normally, she would have stood to receive the Bread and the Wine. She was told to kneel. She rose from the Table anointed with the Spirit and completely healed. We had not been praying for the sick. This

Women's day of praise and prayer – 12th May 1971 – on the way to St. Peter's from the Manor Barn.

work of healing was another gracious sign from the Lord. He had blessed one of His daughters. At the same time, He had reassured us that all we had sought to do that day was in the centre of His will.

There was much food for thought. I began to see how enormous the potential for the release of God's power could be if only His people were free to meet at His Table together. I also began to understand why for this particular day we had been led away from the locally accepted interdenominational centre at Ashburnham. We had celebrated Communion in the church with the oldest origins in the area, side-stepping traditional divisions. We had returned to our common roots. How would the Lord lead in the future?

Chapter Eight

The Vision for the Servants with Jesus

"He appointed twelve, to be with Him " Mark 3:14

"I see! I understand!"

I began to catch a glimpse of the significance of several happenings of recent months. I could see that a number of threads were coming together to show me some of God's pattern for the future. The loose ends at the back of the tapestry were decreasing! I was sitting on my veranda, looking across the garden to St. Peter's church in the distance. A train of thought started.

First I reflected on a recent visit of the Mary Sisters. The day before was a Sunday and the Feast of St. James the apostle. Two of the Sisters had been staying in the area for a few days. In the afternoon, Christians had gathered on Beachy Head to sing praises round the Sisters' praise plaque. While they distributed Christian literature, we sang some of their songs and a selection of the new East Sussex songs. We then returned to Bexhill for Evensong at St. Peter's, where Sister Joy preached. Michael, Beatrice and the Sisters returned to my home for supper. By the end of the day, I had a deep sense that the Lord was calling me to take a new step. It seemed He wanted to bring to birth a new community, bearing His Name. The details of this commission were unclear.

Secondly, I began studying the Bexhill Charter for the first time. As I did so a number of things unfolded. I was reading a special edition produced by Michael in preparation for the twelve hundredth anniversary of the town. I was surprised to discover that Old Town Bexhill was the heart of a very extensive piece of land, given by King Offa to Oswald, Bishop of Selsey. The land stretched from Icklesham to the edge of the Pevensey Marshes. The purpose of the gift was 'to serve the praise of God and the honour of the saints'. Local Bexhill Christians were given eight hides of land to provide for their families. The signing of Offa's famous Charter was the first recorded moment of Bexhill's history. Offa wrote, 'This Charter was written in the year 772 from the incarnation of our Lord Jesus Christ .... on the fifteenth day of the month of August.

I, Offa, King of the Mercians, as the power was conceded to me by God who reigns, have confirmed this Charter of gift, signing it with my own hand, and placed the sign of the Holy Cross'.

What an occasion that must have been. A remarkable number of church and civic dignitaries were present. The Charter was signed by three kings – the King of the Mercians, the King of Kent and the King of the West Saxons – the Archbishop of Canterbury, four bishops and four aldermen also signed.

As I absorbed the contents of the Charter, I began to see why the Lord had led us away from Ashburnham to celebrate His Crowning Day. He had taken us to the Bexhill Manor which, apart from a short break at the time of the Norman Conquest, had belonged to Sussex Christian leaders until the Reformation. The Bishops of Selsey and Chichester lived there when they were ministering in the eastern part of their diocese. The famous Richard of Chichester would have walked frequently between his manor house and St. Peter's church. I could see that the manor site was holy ground. For about eight centuries it had been the centre of Christian leadership for the undivided Church in the East Sussex area. I saw that a part of the Lord's preparation for Revival, was the re-occupation of the site by Christians of all traditions. Christians needed to be living there.

The only suitable building left for restoration and habitation was the old Coach House and servants' quarters. These were described later in the local press as 'a mouldering pile!'. I knew that they must be recovered so that Christians from all traditions could come to pray and meet there with God and each other. The Coach House was to be a catalyst for helping Christians to experience the unity which Jesus had made available.

Already astounded by so much that was unfolding, a third line of thought developed as I started to read the Old Testament lectionary reading set for the day, taken from Chapter 31 of the Book of Proverbs. This passage described the ideal wife. She was a most industrious lady, attending to the welfare of her family and able to provide for the poor and needy. She was a good business woman, buying land and providing clothing and shelter for her whole household. Her husband and children praised her. At the gate of the city where her husband conferred with the elders, he was greatly respected because of her efficiency. She clothed herself in purple.

As I read, a vision began to form of a community of women, devoted to the Lord as their spiritual Husband. They were to live their lives in such a way that He would be honoured by others. Like the Proverbs wife, they would wear purple so that they could be identified as belonging to each other. They would also wear a gold cross as a sign that they were prepared to take up the Cross daily to follow Jesus. At the heart of the vision, was a call to live in a close and intimate relationship with the Lord. They were to be a company of women, called by the love of Jesus, into a fellowship whose main purpose would be to worship Him and comfort Him with their love. Out of this relationship, ministry to others would flow.

My mind was then taken back to the 'Crowning Day' when women from different Christian traditions had been anointed for ministries. I could see they were the first of many who would be called and gifted by the Lord, to take up their ministries and roles within His church. Amongst them, would be those who would also be called to join the new community. By praying and being together, they would become an instrument of unity and understanding between the different church traditions, while at the same time being actively involved and exercising their ministries within their own church fellowships.

I was filled with wonder at the scope of the vision and knew it was a work that only God Himself could bring into being. The calling would be threefold – first and foremost a call to live closely to Jesus; secondly, a call to run a home for the glory of the Lord and where His peace and help could be found; thirdly, a call to discover and use the ministry God was giving.

I could see that step by step the Lord had already been preparing me personally to respond to His vision. For nearly seven years, He had been drawing me closer and closer to Himself. He had given me a home where I was free to do whatever He asked. I had previously been anointed for the ministry of the Word and prayer. The new community would have its' birth in my home. There I would begin to work out my 'Proverbs wife' role. However, I knew right from the beginning that eventually this role, for me, would be fulfilled by making a new home for the Lord and His people at the Coach House in the Manor Gardens!

As I looked up at my garden, the Holy Spirit seemed to confirm, through God's creation, that I was thinking along the right lines. There were eight different purple flowers growing in the garden – sweetpeas, candytuft, stocks, fuchsias, cranesbill, buddleia, hydrangeas and erigerons!

My next step would be to share with my 'Wise men', Eva and others, all that had been revealed so that they could pray with me about the future.

Chapter Nine

Sharing the Vision

"I am among you as One who serves". Luke 22:27

"You will be called by My Own new Name!"

These words came into my mind as I was praying about a name for the new community. I started to read the set scriptures for the day. I was reading a passage from St. Mark's Gospel: James and John had asked Jesus to give them places on His right and left when He came into His Kingdom. All the disciples then began to quarrel amongst themselves as to who would be the greatest. Jesus rebuked and challenged them, "Whoever would be first among you, must be slave of all. For the Son of Man also came not to be served, but to serve and to give His life as a ransom for many". Mark 10:44-45.

A train of thought began to develop in my mind: Jesus' Name was Servant – we are to be called by His new Name – we are to serve with Him – we are to be known as 'Servants with Jesus'. When I shared the vision of the 'Servants with Jesus' Community with Eva, she made a positive response. We went together to inspect the Manor site.

Two days later, I was sitting in my kitchen having breakfast. I was beginning to have 'cold feet' and doubts. Could I be making everything up? It would be most reassuring if I could have some visible, material indication that I was on the right path and in the centre of God's will. As I was thinking these rather negative thoughts, Eva arrived with four gold crosses and chains. She had inherited them from her Aunts, whose family had been goldsmiths. We placed a cross on each other as a token of our commitment to be Servants with Jesus.

Later that day I went to share the vision with Michael and Beatrice. Their response was very encouraging. Michael commented, "When the Lord wants to draw attention to a truth or something that needs doing, He has always worked through groups of people, going back as far as the apostles".

I gradually came to understand the significance of this remark. We were to be a kind of prophetic sign, showing the priority for every Christian to live their lives with Jesus. In such a relationship each Christian could discover their particular ministry and calling. This was so for the apostles and had been for Christians of integrity throughout the ages. At the beginning of His public ministry, Jesus called twelve disciples to be with Him, Mark 3:14. As they shared life with Jesus, they discovered God's will for their lives.

As Mayor's chaplain, Michael knew a number of Bexhill councillors well, as friends. He offered to enquire whether they had any plans for the future use of the Coach House. He discovered that the Council intended to defer making a decision, until more was known about the timing and building of the bypass around Bexhill Old Town. In the meanwhile, Michael suggested that, during the coming year, we should concentrate on working out our new discipline of life.

The Lord had already prepared John to respond to the 'Servants with Jesus' vision. In his praying for East Sussex, he had received complementary insights. One of these, he had shared on 28th June at the monthly Ashburnham meeting which now took place in the setting of a Communion service presided over by John. He based the ministry of the Word on a passage from the book of Deuteronomy about cities of refuge. He could see a time of increasing conflict ahead, especially for those in Christian leadership and ministry. He could see the influence of materialism, secularism and the powers of darkness growing and clashing sharply with the life of God that was coming into so many lives through the Spirit. Some would be wounded in the battle and would need to withdraw to a place of refuge for security, refreshment and prayer. John believed that the Lord had been calling him to create such a refuge at Ashburnham in the old stable block. He also thought that God would raise up other cities of refuge throughout East Sussex.

When John heard about the vision for the Servants with Jesus and the restoration of the Coach House in the Manor Gardens at Bexhill, he thought this could well be one of these cities. He also recognised the tremendous potential of small interdenominational groups of women, covenanted to pray with one another for their immediate local area. He encouraged us to explore further but emphasised that everything needed to be tested by other members of Body of Christ.

At the beginning of August, John invited Ian and Phyllis McCulloch, Eva and myself to join him in working out the details for a night of prayer for East Sussex, which was to be held in October. Ian and Phyllis were from a Brethren background and had worked as missionaries in Paraguay and the Argentine. They had returned to Eastbourne to look after Phyllis' father. In recent years they had received an anointing of the Holy Spirit which had transformed their lives. Ian was one of a small group of ministers who had been meeting monthly with John to listen to the Lord and pray for East Sussex. As we talked and prayed about the preparations for the night of prayer, John and Ian shared two visions given to John and Edmund at their July meeting.

John's vision was of two streams flowing down a mountainside. As they joined together, the water was being controlled by a huge dam, stretching across a valley. One of the streams was rushing down the mountainside, leaping over rocks to reach its destination. The other stream was moving slowly and had almost been brought to a standstill by a barrier of debris blocking the way. As the water piled up behind the barrier, it gave way and flowed to join the other stream.

John gave us his interpretation of the vision which the others had carefully weighed. 'The stream rushing towards the dam represented the Spirit-filled women of East Sussex. The other stream represented Christian men whose progress was blocked by fear and unbelief. As the men opened themselves more and more to the Holy Spirit, the emotional blocks would be swept away'. John felt it was important for Christian men and women of East Sussex to be working more closely together if God's purposes were to be fulfilled. The dam represented the Church which the Lord was building and shaping to fulfil His plans. His Church rightly built and fitting together would be a great blessing to many people, helping them to find God, as the waters of the Spirit flowed! A weak and disobedient Church would be overwhelmed by the presence of God's Spirit and fail to hold back the flood of God's judgement. If the Church failed to fulfil its mission, the world would spiritually drown. It was as the Church kept the Cross in the centre of her life, that God's purposes would be accomplished.

John explained that the framework of a dam is held together by concrete, made of sand, stones, water and cement. He saw the Christian women of East Sussex as sand made of broken stones, the men as stones, the water as Baptism and the cement as the Lord's Supper. The Gospel sacraments of Baptism and Communion were needed to bind all Christians together in the life of the Spirit.

Edmund's vision was of a map of East Sussex. There were small flames of fire dotted about the map. Some were being extinguished, others quenched. Glass bell jars were being placed over the flames that remained, to protect them. The brothers agreed an interpretation of this vision. 'The flames were small groups of women who had been baptised in the Spirit. Some had met with so much opposition that their ministries were being quenched and in some cases, extinguished. The bell jars represented Christian men whose calling was to encourage and protect the women as they sought to serve God and do His will'.

Both of these visions spoke to me. They seemed to complement all that was unfolding about the Servants with Jesus. The role of the Servants within God's overall plan was becoming clearer.

Edmund, however, was not sure that his vision of lights related exclusively to the Servants with Jesus. He knew that the lights referred to the Spirit-filled women but was not prepared to limit what he had seen to the Servants. As far as I could understand his thinking, the activity of the Spirit should not be limited to such a narrow interpretation. We should not put ourselves into bondage and in so doing, lose our freedom in the Spirit.

Towards the end of August, I met with my three wise men in John's family flat at Ashburnham, hoping for their full blessing to begin making the Servants with Jesus' vision a reality. Edmund was unable to give his blessing at this stage. It seemed that in such an important matter, we should be united. We therefore agreed not to go public for the time being. In spite of this setback, Eva and I continued to pray as though we were expecting the vision to be fulfilled. We were shown a number of steps to take so that when the time came to move forward, we would be prepared.

Firstly, we were shown that we were to share the Servants with Jesus' vision with twelve East Sussex women. We were both given the same names in four groups of three. These Christian women came from four different geographical areas. Throughout the autumn, we had the opportunity to speak to all of them in turn. We encouraged them to pray about the vision and asked them to get in touch with us, if they had any insights.

Secondly, we felt the need to have an exploratory discussion with Bexhill's Town Clerk. I arranged to meet him at the end of October. A few days before we met, about one hundred and forty people gathered for the planned night of prayer for East Sussex at Ashburnham. The evening began in the Great Hall. Sister Eva had shared with John a vision of the Hall full of praying people seated in the arms of a cross laid out in red carpet. Over the vision was written: "Stat Crux Dom Volvitur Orbis". The night ended with a Communion service in the parish church. The intercessions at this service took the form of extempore prayer. People in the congregation were free to pray for needs in East Sussex. I offered a short prayer for the future of a piece of land in the county which could have significance for God's work. As soon as I had prayed, a Baptist minister from Hastings stood and spoke prophetically, using words which God had spoken to Joshua as he was about to enter the Promised Land, "Every place that the sole of your foot will tread upon, I have given to you".

This word was used to give me confidence that my interview with the Town Clerk would be good – and it was! He was very interested in our propositions and saw that our plans could be of real benefit to the local community. He offered to approach the Mayor and the chairman of the Planning Committee on our behalf. He also agreed that we could have the key to the Coach House to explore and examine the building with an architect. This we did ten days later together with John.

The third step we took during the autumn with John's encouragement was to consult a solicitor. We needed to know what our legal commitments would be. John showed us the trust deeds of the Ashburnham Christian Trust to give us some idea of the range of things that needed to be considered. He also arranged for me to meet Derek Warren, his own solicitor, who had set up the

Ashburnham Trust. On 10th December, I visited Derek Warren at his office in London This was a very helpful meeting. He suggested that, as we proposed to buy or lease property, we should appoint Christian trustees who had business experience and administrative gifts. We should think about the contents of a constitution as we would need to register with the Charity Commission. The constitution should include our aims. These should be broadly based, making it possible for us to carry out anything we might wish to do in the future. He also advised us to make it very clear that the spiritual affairs of the Community should remain in the hands of the Servants with Jesus themselves. The trustees' responsibilities should be financial and legal affairs. It might too be wise to appoint pastoral advisers from amongst the local ministers and clergy who could act as liaison between the Servants and the general public.

In the light of Derek Warren's advice, we decided to invite three Christian men to become trustees, when the time came for forming of the Servants with Jesus' Trust. John agreed to act as a trustee. During the first week of January 1972, I visited Michael Warren at Barcombe. He agreed to pray about our invitation and said he would make a final decision after the contents of our constitution were known. Later that week, Eva and I visited Douglas Chamberlain at Mayfield. He was eager to do all he could to help us and would willingly be a trustee.

So much progress was being made that John invited Michael, Edmund, Douglas and me to meet with him in his flat. We wanted to know if we had the green light to go forward together to form the new association. Edmund still was unable to give his blessing. Once again, it seemed right to wait. I was bitterly disappointed. Michael returned with me to Bexhill in my car. He was most concerned for my welfare. He said something like this, "Don't let what has happened put you out of action! Don't behave as though they have killed your baby!" Something stirred inside me and I found myself spontaneously saying, "They haven't! The baby has been born! The only problem is that the parents are not agreed about how to bring it up."

After a pause of several weeks we all met once more. This time Eva joined us. After a prolonged and inconclusive discussion, we prayed for guidance. After a very long pause, Eva shared a scripture reference which she had seen in her mind's eye, written across a window – 1 Corinthians 15:58. She had hesitated to share this, thinking, "Surely no chapter in the Epistles has as many as fifty-eight verses? If there is no such verse, the men will be justified in thinking we could be wrong about the Servants with Jesus' vision." As Eva spoke out the reference, Edmund immediately quoted its contents, "Therefore my beloved brethren, be steadfast, immovable, always abounding in the work of the Lord, knowing that in the Lord your labour is not in vain."

The meaning for us all was unmistakable! To hear these words was such a relief. They set us free to take positive actions.

Chapter Ten

Planning for the Future

"I know the plans I have for you.....to give you a future and a hope."
Jeremiah 29:11

There was much work to be done. Explorations, discoveries and events of the last six months were waiting to be consolidated.

First we needed to gather together those women who were being drawn towards the Servants with Jesus. It was important for their calls to be tested and for Eva and myself to be available to answer questions and to pray with them. Several had been anointed for their ministries – one in January, three others from the Hailsham area were anointed by Michael early in February and Ian anointed three Eastbourne women at the end of the month. Another was anointed by John during March in Penhurst church.

We had decided that all new Servants should be known and addressed publicly as 'Sister', followed by their Christian name. This was an important decision, giving a family feel to the new community and emphasising our unity in the Lord. This would also ensure that no distinction would be made between those who were married, single, widowed or divorced. We were to be Sisters equally in the Lord.

Sister Dorothy Mary Osborn of Eastbourne was among those early pioneering Sisters who answered the Lord's call. She was anointed at the end of February for the ministry of intercession. She has written a short testimony of the way her calling to be a Servant with Jesus unfolded:-

"Looking back to the 1970s is a long time. Some missionary friends introduced us to Ashburnham where Cod was working and I remember being given the opportunity to do a research course over nine months under the leadership of Eileen Wheeler, together with my friends, Phyllis and Joyce. This was a real privilege. We understood that several of the Lord's servants in East Sussex had found these very helpful. During this time we found ourselves becoming very close to each other. Days of Prayer and Praise were arranged for the women of East Sussex. One day Eileen, and Eva who had become Eileen's prayer partner, came to see us – that is Joyce, Phyllis and me. They had something to share with us that they believed was from God. They thought He wanted to gather a group of women together to follow the Proverbs' wife way in Proverbs 31 and also in Mark's Gospel where the disciples were to 'be with Him'. They were to wear purple clothes and a gold cross and be anointed for ministry. We well received this, knowing that God was doing all kinds of different things in those days. We were all rather shaken when they informed us that they believed God wanted us to be 'Servants with Jesus' as they were to be called. They left us to consider what they had brought to us. My reactions were first of all, that belonging to an Evangelical Church who discouraged the use of jewellery, let alone a cross, I couldn't do it, no way. Anointing was not accepted for service – What would my husband say? Let alone the Elders, and all my friends at the Church. There was much heart searching and prayer as we considered this. At this moment in time I was reading the book of Ecclesiastes and was very surprised and challenged to read in chapter 9, verses 7-10, words which seemed to be straight from God to my heart. 'Go eat your bread with enjoyment and drink your wine with a merry heart for God has already approved what you do. Let your garments be always white; let not oil be lacking on your head. Enjoy life with the wife (husband), whom you love, all the days of your life He has given you – because that is your portion in life and your toil - Whatever your hands find to do, do it with all your might.' Soon after this I was praying and found myself singing a little song to the Lord.

> 'Jesus, You are Lord of all,
> Jesus, I have given You all,
> Jesus, how I love Your call.'

I stopped abruptly and to confess I didn't love this call to be a Servant with Jesus, and if this was what the Lord wanted, would He please give me that love and also prepare me and my husband to understand. When I, very apprehensively, told John he, immediately, said, 'if this is what God is calling you to, you must obey. I have no objection and will back you all the way.'"

Sister Dorothy Mary

Every Sister could testify to their own personal call. Each has a different story to tell of how God spoke to them, of how He broke through their initial reservations, drew them close to Himself and opened the path for them to obey.

From this time I began to make plans for living at the Coach House. Praying and working for this event became one of my priorities. For over a year, I had been regularly attending the early Communion service on Saturday mornings at St. Peter's. I frequently went straight from the service to spend time quietly in the Coach House stableyard. These were very special times. No workmen or gardeners were about. I used to sit on the slabs of stone left there by the Parks and Gardens Department, along with many other unused items. The whole area inside the stableyard walls was derelict, with a compost heap and rubbish dump for the whole Manor site to the east of the building. Inspite of the wilderness appearance, there was always a strange beauty about the place. As I sat looking eastwards towards the sun rising over the sea and Galley Hill, the whole area seemed filled with the glory of the Lord and bathed in the warmth and light of God's presence. There was an atmosphere of joy and happiness, inspired by the singing of numerous birds. Sometimes doves from the bird house in the Manor Gardens, circled round and settled on the Coach House roof – a lovely token of the Holy Spirit's gift of peace.

The Servants began to meet once a month in my home from 10.00 am to 3.00 pm. This was a time for reading the scriptures, sharing insights and of praying for one another, for the occupation of the Coach House and for the church in East Sussex. We met in the context of the Breaking of Bread. At our March meeting, Sister Eva shared something she had been shown the previous week whilst praying with Ian, Sister Phyllis and myself. She had seen a picture of a parchment scroll. There were several signatures written at the bottom, which she could not decipher; also a date, 28th June 1972. The scroll was sealed with a red seal, indicating that it must be a legal document. Without weighing the vision adequately, the Sisters jumped to the conclusion that the scroll must represent the deeds of the Coach House.

In the meantime, prospective trustees had been meeting to talk over the contents of the Servants with Jesus' constitution. We agreed to follow the main proposals suggested by our solicitor the previous December, including the advice to appoint pastoral advisers. Michael, Edmund and Ian had all agreed to serve in this capacity. On 10th March, I sent our conclusions to Derek Warren so that he could begin his work of drawing up the constitution and registering with the Charity Commission. The completed constitution arrived at my home on 14th June, ready for signing by the trustees, who had arranged to meet early in July.

At the beginning of May, accompanied by Douglas in his new capacity as a trustee, I made a second visit to the Town Clerk. He was again very sympathetic to our cause. He told us that our application for the use of the Coach House was to be considered at a full Council meeting on 26th June.

He would let us know the results of their deliberations within two days; in other words, by 28th June! Our hopes for success were high.

It was a very great disappointment, when 28th June arrived, to know that our offer to restore and use the Coach House had been turned down. The reason given was that in 1973 the Bexhill Council was to be absorbed into the new Rother District Council. The councillors decided that it would be best to wait until the new Council was formed. The new councillors might well have very different plans for such a strategic site.

Late in the afternoon, that day, I was sitting under a dryer at the hairdressers. I was complaining to the Lord, in the kind of mood sometimes expressed by the Psalmists, "Have we done anything wrong? Why did Sister Eva have the vision of the parchment scroll? Had she got the date wrong?" Then suddenly I remembered the constitution which had been posted through my letter box two weeks earlier. It was held together by a green ribbon and red seal! It was there, at home, waiting for the signatures of the trustees. Why hadn't we seen it before? The scroll in the vision must be our constitution.

Then came a sequence of thoughts, "Today is 28th June – that was the date on the scroll – somehow we must get the signatures of the trustees written on the scroll before midnight!" Michael Warren lived at Barcombe to the west of the county; Douglas at Mayfield to the north; John was in London for the day visiting an eye specialist at Moorfields. Humanly speaking, it seemed most unlikely that all three of these gentlemen would be available that evening to sign the constitution. Sister Eva and I were already committed to meet with someone from Seaford to test her Servants with Jesus' calling.

When I arrived home the telephone rang. It was a very apologetic lady from Seaford. She was caught up in a crisis and it was not possible for her to come to Bexhill to meet us. "Don't worry!" I said. "There is something else that Sister Eva and I should be doing this evening."

I telephoned Michael Warren to explain why I thought the constitution should be signed that day. He agreed and suggested we arrived at Barcombe a little before eight o'clock. Dinner would be finished by that time and he had an evening engagement later. I then telephoned Douglas. He was entertaining the Bishop of Nakuru for the evening. If we could arrive at Mayfield by about nine o'clock, there would be a suitable break in the evening's arrangements for him to read and sign the constitution.

Sister Eva arrived at about six o'clock and I explained all that had happened. We set out on the journey to Barcombe and Mayfield, planning to return home via Ashburnham. We reckoned that by ten o'clock, John would have returned from Moorfields. It was a glorious June evening. The timing of events was perfect. Well before midnight our new constitution had been signed by all the trustees. We had toured round a major part of East Sussex, praying as we went.

On my return home I began to prepare for bed. I was thinking over the events of the day, wondering why it was important for the constitution to be signed by 28th June. I then recollected, "Tomorrow is the climax of St. Peter's patronal festival. It is St. Peter's day. There will be special thanksgivings for King Offa, for the Bexhill Charter and for twelve hundred years of Christian history and witness in Bexhill." I knew I must go to the early morning Communion service and take the constitution with me. A flower festival was in progress as part of the St. Peter's tide celebrations. As I went into the church there was a large flower arrangement of figures just inside the door, depicting King Offa giving the Bexhill Charter to Bishop Oswald of Selsey. The Charter was sealed with a large red seal!

After the service I waited to speak with Michael at the church door. "I have another charter here," I said, showing him our new constitution with the red seal. "Wait until everyone has gone!" he said. When the congregation had left, he took the constitution. We went together to the Communion table. Michael offered the constitution to the Lord, praying for God's blessing on all who would ever be associated with the Servants with Jesus.

The constitution began with a comprehensive summary of the aims of the Servants with Jesus. Advised by Derek Warren, the trustees agreed that our main purpose should be:-

"To advance the Christian Faith throughout all or any parts of the world".

We should achieve this aim by means of four subsidiary aims:-

"To promote and pray for the fellowship of all Christian people.

To establish centres for interdenominational worship and evangelism.

To train people of all ages in Christian discipleship and service.

To distribute and publish Christian literature."

Throughout the early autumn, the Sisters were engaged in preparations to appear in public on St. Andrew's Day, 30th November. We planned to start wearing distinctive purple clothes so that it would be easy to recognise us as Servants with Jesus. We negotiated with Garroulds of London, who specialised in making uniforms. We chose a simple classic-style, light purple dress. We also ordered dark purple cloaks with gold linings.

At the end of September, the usual company of East Sussex prayer warriors met in the Great Hall at Ashburnham for the monthly Communion service. John quoted the words, "He ordained twelve to be with Him." Mark 3:14. He shared a picture he had seen as we had been praying. He saw numbers of men in a tug-of-war, pulling in different directions, hurting their hands but achieving little. A nunlike figure was kneeling nearby in prayer, achieving more than all the efforts of the men. I was greatly encouraged by this revelation. The Spirit seemed to be showing that by the time we reached the robing day on 30th November, there would be twelve ready to be known as Servants with Jesus. It was also a reminder that we should never let our prayer ministry be squeezed out by too much activity, however worthy.

Sister Eva had been living at Ashburnham for some weeks. In the middle of October, John suggested that she joined me in my home so that we could begin preparing for the corporate life of the Servants, when the Coach House became ours.

On St. Luke's Day, 18th October, we held another day of praise and prayer for the women of East Sussex in the Manor Barn. It seemed important to us that we should begin occupying the Manor site with worship, praise and prayer. There was a wonderful unity and freedom in the Spirit throughout the day. Although we were not yet wearing our distinctive purple dress, we shared the Servants with Jesus' vision with the women of East Sussex. Several Sisters who had been anointed for ministries and received their crosses gave testimony to their calling. The key thought for the day was from the book of Joshua, "Sanctify yourselves for tomorrow the Lord will do wonders among you." Joshua 2:5.

St. Andrew's Day arrived and the Servants with Jesus' family met in Penhurst church for our commissioning and robing. Although it was late November, the sun shone throughout the service. There were twelve Servants to be commissioned. To support us were several husbands, our trustees and pastoral advisers. John hosted the service, Michael celebrated Communion, Ian led the intercessions for the Servants and East Sussex; Edmund gave the address.

In his introductory welcome, John reminded us that every part of God's creation had its own special glory, "There is one glory of the rose; one glory of the lily. Each Sister too is different with her own unique personality and gifting. You come from very different backgrounds and traditions. It is important that you remain yourselves, while at the same time, living in the reality of being one in the Lord."

Edmund's address was based on the words of Jesus, "Where two or three are gathered in My Name, there am I in the midst of them." Matthew 18:20.

He spoke of the uniqueness of the service, "Probably no other service like this has ever taken place. You are all drawn together by the renewal of the Holy Spirit but it is important to keep Jesus Christ central. Jesus must be kept in the midst. You must never allow a doctrine, a particular approach, a particular experience, to take the place of Jesus Christ".

We sang a new song of commitment and affirmation, given to Sister Joyce Prentice of Eastbourne:-

> "We will rise up and build the City,
> We shall prosper in the Lord!
> We will rise up and build the City,
> Build the City of our God!
>
> Weep for the desolated City,
> Cry for mercy from the Lord!
> We will rise up and build the City,
> Build the City of our God!
>
> We will build on the sure Foundation,
> Which is Jesus Christ the Lord.
> We will rise up and build the City,
> Build the City of our God!
>
> With joints and bands all knit together,
> A holy temple in the Lord!
> We will rise up and build the City,
> Build the City of our God!"

After the distribution of the Bread and Wine, we all remained kneeling and sang:

> "Thy Way, not mine, O Lord,
> However dark it be.
> Lead me by Thine Own hand,
> Choose out the path for me."

When the service was over, we went out into the sunshine and lovely countryside surrounding Penhurst churchyard. We experienced a brief time of fellowship and rejoicing together, greeting one another in the Name of the Lord. The Sisters were relieved and pleased that our Christian brothers approved of our new distinctive dress. They made complimentary comments and were enthusiastic about our light purple dresses and dark purple cloaks. From now on, Sister Eva and I would answer the telephone, "Servants with Jesus! Can we help you?"

Chapter Eleven

Working, Watching and Waiting

"Still the vision awaits its time.....
If it seems slow wait for it, it will surely come." Habakkuk 2:3

"Wow!"

This was the response of an ex-member of the Grammar School when I answered the telephone, "Servants with Jesus! Can we help you?" As we continued to answer the telephone in this way, extraordinary things happened. We had a wide variety of reactions from our families, friends and members of the wider public. One man dialled our number by mistake. Sister Eva found herself talking to an engineer at the top of a telephone pole! "How do you think you can help me?" he asked, attempting to make a witty reply. "I can help you to know God. I can pray for you", Sister Eva continued. "Oh, don't do that!" he said, fearful, it seemed, that her prayers might be answered.

We discovered that our telephone response conveyed in a very few words the heart of our ministry. People began to grasp that we were available to listen, support, pray and assist. As the Servants went about their daily lives, wearing their distinctive purple dress, caring for their families and friends and taking part in the life of their church fellowships, many questions were asked. We saw the need for a concise card which we could give to people in answer to their queries. So, early in 1973, we produced the first piece of Servants with Jesus literature. On the front of a folded card we put our monogram SJW and our full name. On the back was our address and telephone number so that people could easily contact us. Inside the card were some questions and answers outlining our calling and ministry:-

Who are we?

We are a company of women who have been called by the love of Jesus into a fellowship, whose main purpose is to worship Him and to comfort Him with our love. We are called – first 'to be with Him', and then, to minister to others:

"And He appointed twelve, to be with Him, and to be sent out ...."Mark 3:14

What is the meaning of our monogram?
The 'J' in the middle symbolises that Jesus is the centre of our lives and in the midst of us. We believe He has called us to share in the fellowship of His sufferings as we minister to Him and to the world. When He called us, He reminded us of two of His sayings:
"The Son of man also came not to be served but to serve, and to give His life as a ransom for many." Mark 10:45
"I am among you as one who serves." Luke 22:27

What is our commission?
Our main commission is to work and pray for the furtherance of the love and unity of God's People. We pray with Jesus that we and all His People will be one, so that the world will believe that the Father sent Him. We seek by our praying, living and speaking to lift Him up to the world.

Have Sisters individual responsibilities?
Each Sister responded to a call to a specific ministry. Our service with Jesus is to fulfil these ministries, which include intercession, speaking God's word, the encouragement of other Christians, the deliverance of those held by oppression and the powers of darkness, love and service, the healing of the sick.

How do we live?
Each local group of Sisters meets for worship, praise and intercession, as frequently as possible during the working days of the week. Ministry to others arises out of these times of fellowship together.
During the evenings and weekends Sisters are expected to be involved in the normal activities of the local Churches to which they belong.

The husband of one of the Servants was a printer. He printed the card for us in an attractive and pleasing style and layout.

Some Servants were frequently out and about in East Sussex. Others entertained people in their homes or visited when invited to do so. As we listened to peoples' stories and shared their concerns, we found a number of recurring needs. Many felt isolated, alienated and in need of friendship. Others lacked peace of mind, were fearful or broken-hearted. Some felt that life had little purpose and brought little satisfaction. Many complained that no one understood them, they lacked love and there was no one to share their secrets. Some had burdens of guilt, others were afraid of death.

We longed for everyone who talked with us to leave encouraged and with hope, with some message or promise of God they could make their own. With this in mind, we had several cards printed. Each one had a key theme with two or three lines of thought-provoking ideas and a scripture promise. We wrote about such fundamental truths as – "Jesus satisfies! Jesus gives peace! Jesus is alive! Jesus forgives! Jesus knows you! Jesus is real! Jesus understands you! Jesus loves you!"

We carried these cards around with us in our handbags, pockets or Bibles so that we would always be ready to give a helpful word when it seemed appropriate.

We found singing and praise to be powerful instruments in prayer and decided to collect some of the hymns and spiritual songs we had been given into a booklet. Sister Edna Cole worked hard typing out the words on to skins. Other Sisters duplicated and stapled the pages together. We used the songs regularly at our monthly meetings when all the Servants met at Chantry Avenue, Bexhill.

We also used them at our local meetings and took them with us when we went on praise outings with the Mary Sisters. On these expeditions we sang round their praise plaques and distributed Christian literature at such places as Beachy Head, the Dyke at Brighton, Seaford Head, Firle Beacon and at High and Over overlooking the Cuckmere Valley. This was one of the ways we sought to move with God's calling in preparation for Revival in East Sussex. We sang praises and prayed as we moved around the East Sussex countryside.

John Bickersteth, as our Chairman of Trustees, was a very great encouragement throughout our early years in the public eye. He saw our existence as providing a catalyst for the unity of the people of God in the East Sussex area. He took this part of our calling seriously and gave us openings to get to know some of the East Sussex church leaders. He also wanted us to intercede for them with knowledge and for them to trust us with sensitive matters for prayer. With this in mind, he invited the Servants to attend a four-day conference for East Sussex leaders at Ashburnham. Seven of us took part. The time together was led by a team from the Post Green community in Dorset. They had been drawn together by their mutual understanding of Renewal in the Holy Spirit. We learnt a great deal from their shared wisdom and experience.

The conference was followed by a regular monthly seminar for East Sussex leaders. We became an integral part of these special gatherings. They gave us an insight into some of the things God was doing throughout East Sussex. Relationships of trust were built between ourselves, ministers and clergy. Our ministry of intercession for leaders was stimulated and became real, vital and challenging."

A significant happening for East Sussex took place on 26th July 1973. John called a company of about seventy people to join with him for a Communion service in the derelict stableyard at Ashburnham.

Since 1969 John had been deeply convinced that the Lord wanted the eighteenth century Palladian buildings surrounding the yard and the deserted quadrangle restored. He believed that one day they would become a warm centre for the work of God in East Sussex. He had already shared his thoughts about the stableyard becoming a city of refuge at the monthly East Sussex Communion service in June 1971.

Now John felt that the time had come to share the vision with a much wider group of Church leaders and intercessors from East Sussex. Most of the company gathered, were already members of his minister and clergy seminar group or had attended Bible Research Courses. The majority of Servants with Jesus were present together with some of their husbands. The intention of our meeting was to discover the mind and will of God about the way forward for the stableyard.

John based the plan for the day on events described in Ezra Chapter 3. He arranged for a stone Communion table to be erected close to the pump, built of large stone slabs that had been lying around in the yard. As Ezra encouraged the people to worship the Lord before starting to rebuild the Temple so we were to worship Him and seek His direction before starting to rebuild.

A number of insights were shared as worship and prayer were offered and scriptures read, weighed and applied. By the middle of the afternoon we had concluded that the Lord was calling us to take an immediate course of action. We were to make a continuous offering of prayer by day and night for the next fortnight. The extreme deterioration of the stable buildings made it impossible for this to take place in the stableyard itself. John offered the use of the upper room vestry in Ashburnham church. While these discussions were taking place, Sister Eva had been looking round the group. "We are the only ones free to begin the chain of prayer", she whispered. "Everyone else has work or family responsibilities and must go at the end of the afternoon." An hour or so later, Sister Eva and I started the prayer chain in the upper room. John asked us to be responsible for arranging a rota of East Sussex people to come and pray throughout the fortnight. He also sent his secretary, Barbara Stidwill, to us with a purple file. The intercessors were to use this for recording their thoughts. By the end of this fortnight, it was clear that the stableyard was to become a warm centre for God's people in East Sussex. A small community should be set aside to live in the stable. They would exercise a ministry of love, worship, teaching, reconciliation and intercession. It was to be a place where Christian workers, particularly from East Sussex, who were tired from the daily battle, could come for rest and refreshment." After a break for the late summer, those who met regularly for the monthly Communion service in Ashburnham Place, reassembled on 24th September. During the ministry of the Word, John shared with us his strong conviction that the night of prayer in October 1971 had been a dress rehearsal for the stableyard plans. We were to begin the restoration work by laying down pathways in the form of a cross, as a permanent reminder that the work of Jesus on the Cross was the foundation on which all ministry in the stableyard was to be built. The pump was to be removed. The spring which supplied it with water was to be used instead for a fountain, placed at the heart of the cross. This was to be a symbol of the living water of the Holy Spirit, flowing continuously to strengthen the Lord's people. The cobblestones were to be lifted and reset in the arms of the cross, symbolising the 'living stones' of our Lord's spiritual priesthood, His people in East Sussex renewed by the Holy Spirit.

Subsequently, John asked me to keep a detailed log book for the stableyard in the purple file. He felt it important that corporate decisions and prophetic insights should be recorded at the time they were made and given.

In addition to the activities already described, throughout 1973, the Servants with Jesus were involved with numerous concerns for the growth of God's Kingdom in East Sussex. A major commitment was helping with the preparations for the Christian tent at the South of England Show at Ardingly. Throughout the show, several Servants and their husbands had a very fruitful and challenging time talking with people about the Christian faith. The Sisters were invited to lead a day on the ministry of healing at the parish church at Sayers Common. The Bexhill Servants accepted an invitation to lead morning worship and speak at Rye Methodist church.

In October Sister Eva and I were invited by Michael and Gillian Warren to pray with them in their home in Barcombe. They had a special project in mind and were seeking to know the Lord's will. Michael had an old barn in the middle of his fields. He and Gillian had been wondering whether they should move the barn into their garden and convert it into a centre where Christians could meet for conference, prayer, teaching and refreshment. As we prayed together we had a strong conviction that the barn was to be used for the glory of God. We considered Jesus' parable about the Ten Pounds and concluded that the plans for the refurbishment of the barn would be good stewardship in the light of all the Lord was doing in East Sussex. In my mind was also the thought that this could be another city of refuge.

Throughout 1973 however, uppermost in the minds of the Servants was our occupation of the Coach House in the Manor Gardens, Bexhill. We knew that we should not approach Rother District Council officially until later in the year. It was important to give the council members and officials time to settle down to their new responsibilities after the Bexhill Council had been absorbed into the larger local authority. There were two main areas which needed our prayer and attention. One was preparation for our future corporate life at the Coach House; the other the timing and manner of our approach to the Council.

It was Sister Eva and I who had to wrestle with the first issue. Learning to live together was not an easy matter for either of us. We are told by our friends that we are both strong characters and we had both been used to running our own households. Sister Eva's temperament and intercessory ministry meant that she liked to spend much quality time on her own; by nature I am gregarious and enjoy plenty of company. Early on in our living together, we arranged the dining room so that it could be used as a sitting room. We were then able to entertain and listen to people separately or together, depending on the needs of the visitors. This was an important step as we were shown that more and more people would be coming to our home until we moved into the Coach House.

We had to learn to share the use of a car. This had its problems as, although we frequently went on missions together, we often needed to go in different directions. We learnt a great deal about the Lord's guidance and provision through this situation. We found that when we did not know what to do, often someone would offer one of us a lift to our destination. By August the situation was becoming more complex and difficult as both of us seemed to have more and more commitments. I remember praying earnestly and specifically for help. One morning towards the end of September we were expecting someone to coffee who had asked to see us. When he arrived he suggested we went outside before we served the coffee. There, parked in front of the house, was a car which he had bought for the Servants with Jesus. The Lord had revealed to him that Sister Eva and I needed a car each if we were to do our work efficiently. We registered both cars in the name of the Servants with Jesus.

Gradually the Lord unfolded what it would mean for us to share possessions and have a common purse in the new community at the Coach House. During February we were shown independently, similar steps we were to take with our material assets. We were apart for several days. I was attending the Post Green conference for ministers at Ashburnham. Sister Eva had decided to remain at home to pray. As the Post Green team shared their testimony, I knew that I was to transfer the deeds of the house to the Servants with Jesus. In her time of prayer and waiting on the Lord, Sister Eva was shown that she should transfer her shares to the Servants' account. We shared our thoughts with the trustees at our next meeting. After much discussion, they accepted our propositions and the necessary procedures were set in motion.

Another step of obedience was taken later in the year. Sister Phyllis McCulloch and her husband Ian believed God was calling them to move to Emsworth to pastor a new church and to train Bible students. They had seen a large and suitable house which they believed was the right one for the new enterprise. They did not have the money needed for the deposit. As Sister Eva prayed about the matter, she understood that if we gave Sister Phyllis and Ian £300 from our account, the Lord would release all the money needed for the purchase and would provide for us, when the time came, for the restoration of the Coach House. We telephoned Sister Phyllis and Ian. They were overjoyed. The timing of our call was perfect. They had just finished praying and crying to the Lord for His provision and guidance. Within a few weeks, they had purchased the house.

Sister Eva and I met daily every weekday with our other two Bexhill Sisters for worship and prayer. We started at nine o'clock and spent an hour together. Much prayer was made, particularly for the Lord's people in Bexhill and for the possession of the Coach House. On St. Luke's day we were shown that we were to set aside our small box room as a prayer room where we could hold our times of corporate prayer and be able to pray with visitors. We went to work immediately, cleaning and refurnishing the room.

Sister Dorothy Mary Osborn from Eastbourne was greatly burdened to pray about the Coach House. From time to time she came to Bexhill to pray on the Manor site with us. One memorable occasion was at the end of March when Sister Dorothy McGill, Sister Eva and myself joined her in the late afternoon. The gardeners had gone home. We went into the derelict yard and prayed prayers of faith for the land which we believed God was giving us. Sister Dorothy Mary based her prayers on some scripture promises from the book of Isaiah:

> "Look upon Zion, the city of appointed feasts! Your eyes will see Jerusalem, a quiet habitation, an immovable tent, whose stakes will never be plucked up, nor will any of its cords be broken. But there the Lord in majesty will be for us place of broad rivers and streams........"
> Isaiah 33:20-21.

The monthly meetings of all the Sisters at Chantry Avenue were of prime importance in praying about the occupation of the Coach House site. We finished our May meeting early and went on a prayer expedition to the walled garden, a beautiful part of the Manor site, next door to the Coach House area. All the Servants were present. A gentle rain was falling so there were no visitors or gardeners about. We were free to sing and pray as the Holy Spirit led us. The beauty, quiet and colour of the garden, filled with tulips and wallflowers, made us feel that it was a place created for the glory of God. We were given a strong sense of unity and of the presence and power of the Spirit.

We had another full meeting of Sisters in July when we agreed to ask our trustee, Douglas Chamberlain, to contact Rother District Council about the

Coach House. By this time Douglas had moved from Mayfield to Eastbourne and was close at hand to be more involved in our life and activities. After careful consideration Douglas felt that Sister Eva should make the initial approach to the Council by speaking to the council member for the Old Town ward. His advice should be asked about contacting the Mayor and the chairman of the General Purposes' Committee. Douglas felt that before this was done, all the Sisters should have a time of heart-searching. They should make sure that all their relationships were right and count the cost of moving forward to possess the Coach House land.

Sister Eva's meeting with the Old Town council member was arranged for 29th September, the Feast of St. Michael and all Angels and the fourth anniversary of our commissioning for ministry in East Sussex.

During August and September I spent several long nights on my own in the upper room at Ashburnham as part of the prayer chain. This gave me ample opportunity to prepare personally for the move forward.

On the morning Sister Eva was to meet with the councillor, I went to early Communion at St. Peter's and later spent time praying in the walled garden relinquishing everything to the Lord.

When Douglas heard from the Council at the end of October, it seemed that our application was being seriously considered. The dates of a series of sub-committees was outlined, culminating in a full council meeting on 17th December. After a meeting of the Amenities' Committee, the Mayor came to meet with the Bexhill Sisters in our home. We were planning to celebrate our first anniversary of coming into public on Saturday 30th November on the Manor site. We would start with a celebration of Communion in the Manor Barn. The Mayor gave us permission to go into the Coach House yard after the service to sing and pray.

We joined in our celebrations with expectancy. Our trustees, pastoral advisers, Sisters and their husbands were all present. After Communion we went through gates that led to the Coach House. We sang some of our spiritual songs. As it was St. Andrew's day, we prayed that we would be good evangelists like St. Andrew, when we possessed the land that would one day be ours. The men present knocked on all the doors of the Coach House, claiming future entry.

On the day of the full council meeting, Sister Dorothy Mary telephoned to share a scripture for the day, "Many are the plans in the mind of a man but it is the purpose of the Lord that will be established." Proverbs 19:21.

This verse was a great comfort when we were told several days later that the Council had decided to defer a decision until the Parks' and Gardens' equipment had been moved to the West Station.

Months and years of watching and waiting still lay ahead!

Chapter Twelve

Continuing to Work, Watch and Wait

*"Commit your way to the Lord, trust in Him and He will act....
wait patiently for Him."* Psalm 37:5- 7

    The next three years were some of the most exhausting and demanding I have ever lived through. There were numbers of delightful travelling companions along the path. On the other hand, there were those who had started with me on the East Sussex journey who caused much pain. They distanced themselves until they could be sure that God was leading. The feeling of rejection that resulted was sometimes devastating. In spite of this, the Servants with Jesus as a group, knew that God was with them.

    Sister Eva and I were coping with an ever increasing number of people coming to our home, often to stay for several days. Some of our guests were a great encouragement and inspiration. Others were needy, distressed or seriously disturbed. They drained our emotional and spiritual resources to the limit. Once, when I was praying with other Servants with Jesus, a clear picture came to mind. I saw a multitude of distressed people climbing a hillside to drink from a Communion cup. As they drank, they were comforted, their sorrows were turned into joy and their sadness into singing. It seemed the Lord was challenging us to lay down our lives daily for others so that they would find their comfort and strength in knowing Jesus.

    For several years we experienced a time of intensive training and preparation for our future life at the Coach House. Undergirding everything was our corporate life of prayer. All the Servants continued to meet once a month for worship, prayer, to seek direction from the scriptures and the guidance of the Holy Spirit. Each local group met several times a week for the same purpose.

    A major involvement for most of the Sisters was preparation for the restoration of the stableyard at Ashburnham. There had been very little action since September 1973 when John shared his conviction about laying down the cross in the yard. It was important that this work should begin. One Thursday evening in April 1974, two dozen or so Stable friends met for a Communion service in the Green Room at Ashburnham. After sharing insights from the Old Testament story of Nehemiah rebuilding the walls of

Jerusalem, we concluded that Michael Oldroyd should be set aside to supervise the work of laying down the cross. He was commissioned by the whole body present with the laying-on-of-hands. He was given authority to gather those who had suitable gifts to help with practical work and also those who would share with him in prayer and planning.

Michael went quickly into action. He invited five of us to join him on the following Tuesday. He chose us for our particular giftings. It was not until we came together for the first meeting that it dawned on him that we were all closely connected with the Servants with Jesus. He had chosen one of our prayer partners, Terrell Boyes, one of our trustees, Douglas Chamberlain and three Servants with Jesus – Sister Eva, Sister Peggy and myself. The day after our first meeting, the practical work started. Sister Dorothy Mary, Sister Eva and myself had the privilege, excitement and joy of being the first volunteers to start lifting the cobbles. A few weeks later, Gordon Labbett was also invited to join the team, bringing with him his mechanical digger and building expertise. We became known as the Stable Planning Group. The word of the prophet Haggai became our working brief: "Be strong, all you people of the land and work. For I am with you, declares the Lord". Haggai 2:4 We believed that the laying down of the cross was to be a continual reminder that in everything we undertook we were to lift up Jesus. The men of the group quickly set to work to create a temporary room in the centre of the Stable coach house with very flimsy polythene walls. This was to provide a place for prayer, worship and listening to God in the midst of all the bustle and activity of the demolition and restoration work. The monthly East Sussex Communion services were transferred from the house to this room which also became the venue for the weekly meetings of the Planning Group. A Saturday volunteer working party was quickly formed to help lift cobbles and execute a variety of tasks. The work force consisted mainly of the Planning Group, eight or so Servants with Jesus and their husbands.

Before the foundations of the cross were laid, the old pump and horse drinking-trough were removed from the centre of the yard. This left a spring bubbling up where the centre of the cross was to be. Michael had discovered an old fountain in the kitchen gardens. This was put in place to channel the spring waters. The fountain was to remind all who visited the Stable that effective living and working for the Lord could only be achieved through the life-giving, refreshing, enabling Holy Spirit.

After the foundations had been laid, the work of creating the cross as it is seen today, began. The outline of the cross was made with red bricks taken from the apron of bricks that had surrounded the original pump. This was filled in with small rectangular briquettes from the old stable floors. They were set in a pattern of seven lines of herring-boning to remind us of the Lord's seven words from the Cross.

By the time we met for the December Communion service, the laying down of the cross had been completed. Earlier in the month the barrier was removed which had been erected across the main gateway on the northside of the stableyard while the work was in progress. John then led us in prayer asking that the whole stableyard area would be filled with the love and light of Jesus and that all who entered would come to know Him as the Way, the Truth and the Life. All who wished to do so could now enter the yard by the foot of the cross.

Much thought was given to the future use of the buildings and the vision for a community to run the day-to-day ministry of the Stable. A few church leaders who were deeply committed to the Stable project sometimes joined John and the Planning Group to pray and consider this matter. As we met together we reached the following conclusions:-

"Firstly, the coach house on the southside of the stableyard was to be the spiritual centre for the Stable ministry. The ground floor room would be the main worship room. The upstairs rooms would provide smaller rooms for personal ministry, teaching, prayer and study.

Secondly, the east wing of the building should be suitable for families living Spirit-filled lives.

Thirdly, the west wing was to be a hospitality wing, with provision for about a dozen resident guests and catering facilities for much larger groups who would come on day visits to use the coach house. There should be one family unit in this block, whose special responsibility would be to care for the physical needs of the visitors and be in charge of the catering.

At the beginning of 1976, the cobbles which had been lifted from the old stableyard in 1974, were still piled in four enormous heaps in the yard. In April the Planning Group were shown clearly how the cobbles were to be relaid. Through the phrase from Ephesians 6:16, "Above all, taking the shield of faith" we realised that the cobbles were to be set in the form of a shield as a background to the cross. The Spirit showed us that the cross and the cobbles together were to give the impression of being designed as a Crusader shield. This was a particularly exciting revelation as it solved the geometrical problems that had presented themselves every time we had discussed the re-laying of the cobbles!

In this way the final piece of Stable prophetic symbolism was unfolded. The cobbles would become the symbol of all the 'living stones' of East Sussex, joined to the Lord, the chief Corner Stone and to one another to form a shield of faith as they prayed.

For me personally, there was another important feature of the waiting years before the Coach House in Bexhill was released. It was a time of considerable inner tension. I was involved closely with three churches of different traditions. I was a member of Beulah Baptist Church. On Saturday mornings I attended the Communion service at St. Peter's Bexhill. I was frequently at Ashburnham parish church for early Communion on Sundays. My wise men gave their blessing to this routine, recognising the ecumenical nature of my calling. This was an enriching experience but also provoked hostility. Negative reactions came from those who did not seem able to respond to the way the Holy Spirit was drawing together Christians from very different backgrounds. I began to catch a small glimpse of the pain the Lord suffers through the divisions of His Church.

In this situation Michael Townroe gave me words of wisdom on two different occasions. His remarks helped me to come to terms with so much that was going on around me. "You are involved in something much bigger than can be contained in one church," he said. Later he advised, "Don't waste one ounce of emotional energy worrying about church allegiance!" His words seemed to be the voice of God, removing anxieties and a spirit of self-condemnation. However perplexing the various tensions and pressures at the time, I knew that I was in the centre of God's will.

Subsequently one November morning in 1975, previous events and insights began to come together in my mind like threads being woven into a pattern. I was taken back to an East Sussex Communion service which John had celebrated sometime ago in the Ashburnham Library. As he blessed the bread, I had seen a small white loaf. It seemed that an invisible knife cut it into three triangles. The bottom of the loaf formed the base of a foundation triangle. The other two sides of this triangle were equal in length and joined to form a point above the centre of the base. These two equal sides each formed a base for the other two triangles. As the knife cut along both these base lines, it was as though two invisible hands were waiting to receive the two separate parts. The hands then gently placed the triangles back into place.

I did not understand the vision at the time. The impression was very vivid. I felt the vision should not be lost so I described what I had seen to John before going home.

So it was months later, as I was praying, the vision returned. The loaf was whole. On the foundation triangle was written the word 'Catholic', on the triangle to the left "Pentecostal', on the triangle to the right 'Protestant'. Above the loaf was written, 'One holy catholic apostolic church', below the loaf, 'One Loaf! One Body! Praise My Name!'

As I pondered on what I had seen, the current popular perception of the three churches I knew so well came to mind – St. Peter's as Catholic, Beulah

THE LOAF VISION

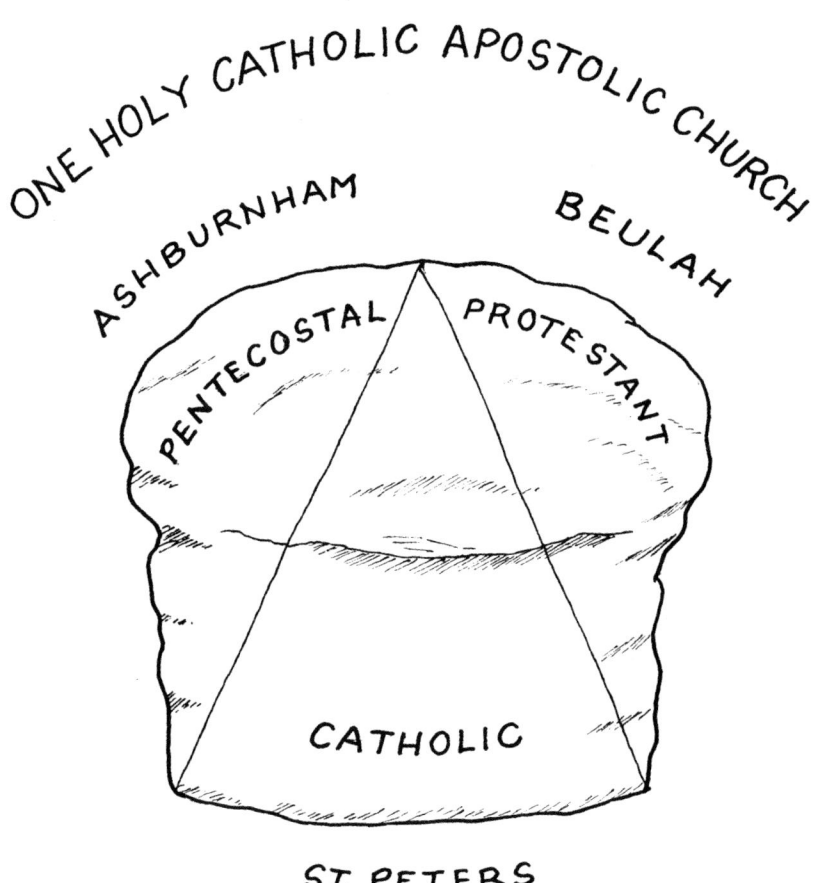

ONE HOLY CATHOLIC APOSTOLIC CHURCH

ASHBURNHAM BEULAH

PENTECOSTAL PROTESTANT

CATHOLIC

ST. PETERS

ONE LOAF! ONE BREAD! PRAISE MY NAME!

Illustration by Sister Jean Warren

as Protestant and Evangelical, Ashburnham as Pentecostal. I then saw that for any local church to be complete, there needed to be within it an interweaving of all three traditions. I also saw that this was already beginning to take place in the three churches mentioned.

God was doing a new thing in His Church. He was making all things new, drawing His people closer together through the work of His Spirit. Many things in the Church were being shaken and would continue to be so until only those things remained which really mattered and could never be shaken.

My wise men all responded positively to what some of us have come to call 'The Loaf Vision'. It made such sense and helped us to understand some of the things that were happening. John, in particular, frequently made reference to it. Knowing that the heart of my ministry and that of the Servants with Jesus was the drawing of God's people together, he often enquired, "Eileen, have you done any loafing' recently?"!

Chapter Thirteen

Action for Restoration

"Whatever your hand finds to do, do it with your might." Ecclesiastes 9:10

"There are two Servants with Jesus sitting in the public seats. They must not speak, but if their association is still interested in occupying the Coach House, please will they nod!"

These words were spoken by Councillor Beard, chairman of Rother District Council's Amenities' Committee. The councillors had been discussing the future use of the Coach House in the Manor Gardens. A reference was made to the Servants with Jesus. One of the councillors had just commented, "Surely these ladies have found somewhere else to do their work by now?"

Sister Eva and I had heard this meeting was to take place so decided to attend, dressed in our distinctive purple. It proved most important that we were present. We were able to nod vigorously. As a result, the interest of the Servants was included in the discussion that followed. This exchange in January 1976 was the signal that our main efforts and prayers were now to be concentrated on obtaining the Coach House.

We were to experience during the following months a most wonderful interweaving of events. To some, they may appear to have been coincidences. To us they gave an assurance that God was with us and guiding. For example, one afternoon in March I came to face to face with Councillor Beard in the foyer of the De La Warr Pavilion. He started the conversation and offered advice about how to proceed to occupy the Coach House.

Christian friends and contacts were used to give us much encouragement, sometimes far beyond their own immediate understanding. One such person was our friend, Terrell Boyes. He came to stay with us for a time at the beginning of April after spending several months in Israel. He brought with him a gift of twelve small wooden crosses from Jerusalem, one for each of the Sisters. This gift had special meaning for us as, for sometime we had thought of the Coach House as our Jerusalem, a place where we believed God's peace was going to be seen and experienced. This unexpected gift was a lovely token, pointing us towards our God-given goal.

Before Holy Week, we were busy writing a leaflet in plain, everyday English about the Coach House and our intentions. We wanted to have something about our plans to give to councillors, church leaders and all who made enquiries. We also wanted to give them an opportunity to ask questions and to visit us if they so wished.

Holy Week itself was a special time of spiritual preparation as we recalled the story of Jesus going up to Jerusalem. Canon Derek Allen, who had recently come to East Sussex, led daily meditations at St. Peter's. His ministry helped to renew us in the Holy Spirit. Michael Townroe suggested that we invited Father Derek to our home, to talk about our community and ideas for the Coach House. There was a wonderful richness in the fellowship we shared. He brought with him a sense of peace and warmth and blessing for the future. This was the beginning of a relationship which, in later years, was going to have a considerable effect on my own Christian journey.

Michael planned a time of ministry for renewal to take place soon after Easter. The venue was St. Peter's and the Manor Barn. He invited Dr. Denis Ball of the Post Green community to lead us on the theme, 'From Fear to Freedom'. We experienced healing and much blessing. Michael suggested that he, Beatrice and some of the Servants with Jesus should take the opportunity to meet with Denis to talk about community life. He thought Denis would have valuable things to share with us about the joys and hazards of communal living. We met in our home. Denis was down to earth and practical, pointing out pitfalls to be avoided. During a time of prayer, he spoke a prophetic word, encouraging us to go forward with the Coach House vision:

> "Don't be afraid of the dark.
> Don't be afraid of those who would discourage.
> Don't be afraid of the high walls.
> Don't be afraid of the noise of the enemy.
> When you walk through the valley I will bring you out into a broad place, where I shall set a table for you in the wilderness.
> I will lead you in and out to still waters and green pastures.
> In the valleys, I Your Shepherd will comfort you with My rod and with My staff.
> I will give you your hearts' desires.
> You will dwell in My house and I will anoint you.
> You will sing My praises in Zion and you will manifest My glory.
> Do what I command you and I will lead you out of darkness into light."

Three days of conference finished with a Communion service in the Manor Barn. Michael, Denis and Edmund ministered together. At the end of the service, Denis invited members of the congregation to go forward to pray for them with the laying-on-of-hands. He asked that prayer should be made for God's blessing on their different ministries and callings. The whole evening was a great inspiration. It seemed to be a foretaste of things to come on the Manor site.

There were other encouragements too. We were given several financial gifts towards the cost of restoring the Coach House. I had another helpful conversation with Councillor Beard about procedures. Michael discovered that the editor of the Bexhill Observer had respect for our work and was prepared to publish an article about us.

Then in the middle of May, on my birthday, there was a most unusual sequence of events which increased my faith. A few days earlier, we had met for our bi-annual trustees' meeting. When we had finished the business in hand, John said, "Let us find a suitable date for our next meeting in November". "Surely we need an earlier date?" I said. "I think we shall hear something from Rother District Council before then!" "If we do, we will arrange an extra meeting", John replied, "and we will celebrate with a chocolate cake!"

Several days later, on my birthday, the Bexhill Servants were having their daily prayer time. Sister Eva prayed a rather unconventional prayer, "Please, Lord, may it not be too long before we celebrate with that chocolate cake!"

Immediately the front door bell rang. I went to answer the door. There stood Lily Hall, an elderly member of Beulah, with a chocolate cake she had made for my birthday! She had never given me a birthday present before. "Whatever made you bring me a chocolate cake?" I asked. "Yesterday, I was praying while I was working in my kitchen," she explained. "I was asking the Lord if I should do anything about your birthday. The words, 'Make her a chocolate cake!' seemed to come strongly into my head. So here I am! I am sorry I am so early. I set out to arrive at the end of your prayer time. Someone stopped on the way and offered me a lift. I thought this was a wonderful provision and that you would understand if I interrupted your praying". "The timing of your arrival is perfect," I said, "in fact an immediate answer to prayer! If you had arrived a few seconds later or a few seconds earlier, your gift would not have had the same impact."

I then explained to Lily what had happened. She was thrilled. This event had a profound influence on me. I saw how very important Lily's obedience to a simple, homely instruction had been. She was used to release the gift of faith in me and others, a gift which carried us through the months ahead. From that time, I knew, however long we had to wait, the Coach House would one day be ours.

Lily and the chocolate cake story inspired us to set to work with increased enthusiasm. First we recognised that the time had come to share the vision for the Coach House with a wider circle. It was important that local Christians and members of the general public, particularly those living in the Old Town, should know what was happening. False rumours of our intentions needed to be corrected. With this in mind, we joined the Old Town Preservation Society. We were pleased to discover that a significant number of members regarded our plans favourably. We also distributed the leaflet which we had prepared before Holy Week to all who were interested.

Our second course of action was to consult with the Town Hall officials and engage in conversation with as many councillors as possible. We found the Town Hall officers most co-operative, giving us much helpful advice. An interview was arranged with Mr. Joy on Ascension day. He advised us to write to the administrative secretary at the Town Hall, re-applying for the Coach House. He suggested that we attended the next Recreation and Leisure Committee on 1st June, as the future of the Coach House was on the agenda. He promised to give us a list of members of the committee after the meeting so that we could contact councillors likely to be favourable and keep them fully informed about our activities. He advised that we should write personally to each one, to create a flame of interest which could later be fanned with conversation. He warned us we had a big task ahead in establishing good public relations.

As we entered the committee room a few days later we were given an encouraging and warm welcome by Councillor Waite and by Mr. Hope, the Chairman's and Chief Executive's secretary. The meeting itself was disappointing. A number of councillors seemed to be deliberately making delaying tactics. However, one important decision was made, to go ahead with moving the Parks' and Gardens' equipment from the Coach House to the West Station.

Lily arriving with her cake at exactly the right moment, taught us that daily happenings could be God-incidents rather than coincidences. This was particularly true of our meetings with councillors. We attempted to talk to every councillor either face to face or on the telephone. Special opportunities opened up for communication which were not of our planning.

Councillor Traice was beginning to make plans to provide a home for battered wives in Barrack Hall in the Old Town. She invited Sister Eva, myself and several others to join her in thinking, planning and praying about her project. In this way we grew to know her well and were able to give each other mutual support and advice.

July provided another unique opportunity for communication. The Bexhill Grammar School celebrated the Golden Jubilee of the foundation of boys' and girls' schools in 1926. Councillor Stevens and myself were invited to speak; Councillor Stevens as an old boy of the boys' school and me as an ex-headmistress of the girls' school. We were asked to cut the cake together. More importantly during the evening, Councillor Stevens as the Chairman of Rother District Council, initiated a conversation about the Servants with Jesus' plans for the Coach House. In this relaxed and informal situation, it was possible to convey to him our aims and aspirations. I was able to make it clear that we were hoping to offer service to the whole local community and to be available to listen.

Several councillors came to visit us in our home. Some were most encouraging, others full of questions. Councillor Lewns, urged on by his wife, gave us enthusiastic support. Councillor Weaver, who was the Vice Chairman of the Council and one of the country representatives agreed to support us. He advised us to speak to other country councillors and to make it very clear that we would not be a liability to rate payers

Councillor Carpenter, who was also Mayor of Bexhill, when he knew that Michael Townroe and Edmund Heddle were our pastoral advisers, became a good ambassador for our cause. He had felt it necessary to make sure that we were truly ecumenical. When Councillor Carpenter became Mayor, he had arranged for his civic service to be at Sackville Road Methodist church. Sister Eva and I were present at his service of commitment and were excited when we heard him read his chosen passage of scripture from the first chapter of the book of Joshua. It contained the verse we have been given prophetically five years earlier at the Ashburnham night of prayer, "Every place that the sole of your foot will tread upon I have given you". We were able to share with Councillor Carpenter how encouraging he had been.

Several councillors expressed a fatherly concern for us. They were most anxious that we should understand the responsibilities we were taking on. They wanted to make sure that we would be spending our resources wisely. We had a most lively discussion with Councillor Cooper who visited us for two to three hours. After his visit I often met him when I was out walking my dog and he always wanted to know how we were getting on. Councillor Turnball sympathised with us that affairs were being so long drawn out. He encouraged us to continue our petitions as he thought we would have the Coach House in the end.

Affairs were indeed long drawn out! A few councillors were very opposed to our project. We anticipated that a final decision about the Coach House would be reached at a full Council meeting in December. Instead, it was agreed that others should be given the opportunity to make application to restore and rent the Coach House. Tender documents would be prepared to make this possible. A few days later, the Planning Department at the Town Hall got into touch with us to say that the Council's solicitor was preparing these documents. They were expected to be available during the first week in January 1977 and would need to be returned within four to six weeks.

Councillor Waite kindly called to give us advice and to tell us that there were likely to be three other applicants. We should complete the documents as quickly as possible. Signing the documents would not be a legally binding agreement but rather a declaration of intent, like paying a deposit for a house. We should make an offer of £50 per annum as a rent explaining that, in view of the great expense involved in the restoration work, we hoped for a peppercorn rent. We should make a general agreement to carry out the renovation works required by the Council for the exterior of the building. These were estimated at £27,000. In addition, we would carry out the restoration of the interior, according to our needs. Councillor Waite was of the opinion that we had a considerable amount of goodwill, both amongst the Town Hall officers and the councillors including the Mayor. He was concerned that we should take the maximum advantage of the current situation and get our application in promptly. He was keen that it should be considered by the Recreation and Leisure Committee before the end of the civic year. After 9th May, there would be a new Mayor and the Council's committees would be reconstituted.

We followed Councillor Waite's advice. On the morning of the Recreation and Leisure Committee we received a telephone call from the Town Hall. We were advised not to attend the committee in the evening as councillors who supported us would feel freer to express themselves if we were not present! The next morning Mr. Hope telephoned. He told us that he was not free to speak about anything that had been discussed but he considered things were moving in the right direction for us.

There were still four months to wait before the final battle was won! The councillors were provided with a document to study, prepared by the Planning Department. The outside cover we found most inspiring. It contained an outline sketch of the Coach House and was headed, 'Action for Restoration'! These words were so apt; they summarised all we had in mind for the future, both for the building and the lives of the people we hoped to touch. The inside of the document explained in detail, the layout and condition of the building. It also contained proposals from the Planning Department about suitable uses for the building. They thought the ground floor could be used for the public. The first and second floors should be for residential use as they had not been constructed for heavy traffic. The proposals we had made in our tender document exactly fitted the Planning Department's suggestions.

The last stage of the battle began on 5th July when the newly constituted Recreation and Leisure Committee met. They had the responsibility of making a recommendation to the Council, after studying the tender documents which had been submitted. The full Council would make the final decision on 1st August.

The 5th July was a glorious sunny morning. Between eight and nine o'clock I went to the Manor Gardens to walk the dog and to pray. When I arrived, there were several workmen in the branches of a huge beech tree which, in previous years, had almost obscured the Coach House from view when it was in full leaf. It had died in the 1976 drought. The men were cutting down the tree. For me the timing of this task was perfect. It seemed the Lord was saying, "The time is now ripe for you to have the Coach House. The way is clear and everyone will see My work in progress".

The next morning Councillor Waite telephoned. He had wonderful news. The other applicants had withdrawn and the Recreation and Leisure Committee were recommending to the full Council that the Servants with Jesus' offer for the Coach House should be accepted.

When the full Council meeting took place on 1st August, Michael Townroe, as chaplain to the Council, stayed on after the introductory prayers to listen to some of the debate. I understand from him that this was very lively. There were still a few councillors strongly opposed to the Servants with Jesus' occupation of the Coach House. Others made excellent speeches on our behalf, resulting in a large majority vote in our favour.

Early in the nineteen-seventies Sister Eva had had a dream in which three men arrived at her door with a scroll saying, "We've got the land!" Between half past ten and half past eleven, after the Council meeting had finished, three men 'phoned us in succession, to tell the good news that the Coach House was ours – Mr. Joy, Councillor Lewns and Councillor Waite. A little later Councillor Traice telephoned and said, "It's all over to you now!" In the midst of all the jubilation and joy, the weight of our future responsibility began to dawn.

The Coach House as released to us in August 1977 by Rother District Council.

Chapter Fourteen

Marvellous Provision

".... to Him Who by the power at work within us is able to do far more abundantly than all that we ask or think .... to Him be the glory"
Ephesians 3:20-21

We were now to experience an extraordinary coming together of numerous threads resulting in a beautiful tapestry.

I am not writing about literal threads and cloth, but rather of an interweaving of events, relationships, circumstances, monies, hardwork and material resources which produced a very pleasing and fitting backcloth to the Manor Gardens.

Today, over twenty years on, the official Bexhill brochure describing local attractions says, "During the summer months the Sackvilles' Coach House forms a dramatic backdrop to open-air theatre performances of Shakespeare's plays"!

In one sense this is a most satisfying remark for the Servants with Jesus, as in the 1970's councillors expressed concern that the restoration work should blend in with the environment. It has since been a source of wonder to us that we were able to achieve this. On the other hand, the remark is somewhat misleading, as the Coach House now belongs to the Servants and is open to all members of the public seeking peace and refreshment. We see the Coach House as a part of the spiritual inheritance of everyone living in the area.

There was much rejoicing over the victory won at the August Council meeting. The councillors had agreed that, in return for restoring the Coach House, the Servants with Jesus could lease the property for a period of twenty years at a peppercorn rent. No security of tenure would be guaranteed beyond that time.

In legal terms, the Coach House project was a risk but in the perspective of the Lord's promises totally secure. We concluded that after twenty years, God's purposes for us would either have been completed or it would be obvious to all concerned that the lease should be renewed. Better still, it might be possible by then, for our ultimate hope for the purchase of the Coach House to be realised.

The day after the Council's decision, the good news was shared with trustees, pastoral advisers, friends and prayer partners. The news spread rapidly Numbers of well-wishers telephoned us before we could telephone them!

With the help of our trustees, we immediately set to work to make plans for the restoration. Douglas Chamberlain contacted Peter Evenden, a much respected local architect and surveyor. By the following day, he had accepted our proposition with great enthusiasm. Douglas also arranged with the chief administrative officer for us to have the keys to the Coach House so that we could see over the building. Within a week Sister Eva and I met with them both in the Coach House. Most of the building was in semi-darkness as broken windows had been boarded up. Cobwebs were festooned from the ceilings and walls. There were small pieces of glass lying about and everywhere was dusty and dirty.

Sister Eva and I had decided how the different rooms should be used. The ground floor, with its damp, bricked flooring, originally used for coaches, should be transformed for public use, consisting of a kitchen, dining space, meeting room and cloakroom area. The first floor had been kitchens and living rooms for the servants of the old Manor House; this we planned should become an office and a flat for Servants with Jesus in residence. The second floor had been used for small bedrooms, a hay loft and an attic. We aimed to make the hay loft into a prayer room and the rest of the floor into bedrooms and a bathroom for house guests.

When we shared our ideas with Peter Evenden he thought they were practical. He began work on the plans immediately. It was a lovely surprise when three weeks later, he called on Sister Eva and me on his way home from work, with his draft plans. He thought we might like to study them over the August Bank Holiday!

We had many encouragements throughout August and on into the autumn. Most days we received financial gifts for the work of restoration. This happened in spite of the fact that it was our deliberate policy not to ask for gifts. Then Kenneth Gibson, instigator of the Ashburnham Bible Research courses, visited us. He had been praying for us over a period of time. He was persuaded that the Lord was answering prayers that had been made over many years, for the whole Manor site to be used for the glory of God. He felt that the prayers of the saints of the ages were making their impact. The work which we were about to do, would be a continuation of a work begun many years ago in the time of King Offa and we were not to worry about financial resources.

Peter Evenden worked very hard throughout the autumn, frequently meeting with members of the Planning Department and Mr. Bird, the Council's architect. He gradually obtained permission for all our ideas to be put into practice. He always let us know when significant interviews were taking place so that we could pray. By December, all the details had been settled and there was a final agreement for the plans to be put into operation.

Just before Christmas, Peter Evenden arrived on our doorstep with about seventy pages of work specifications for the Coach House. He thought we would like to study them over Christmas, piece by piece. In the meanwhile, he had sent out copies of the specifications to four possible contractors.

Throughout 1977 the future use of the Coach House had received a high profile in the local press. As a result, several Bexhill Christians approached us offering prayer support and practical help at the Coach House. This was a marvellous, God-given provision, a work force in the making, drawn from different churches in the town, including Beulah Baptist Church, St. Barnabas', St. Peter's, the Pentecostal Church, Sackville Road and Springfield Road Methodist churches. We began to meet together regularly for prayer and to prepare for the time when the Coach House would be open to the public. We sometimes called these supporters "Jerusalem Helpers"; at other times "Seventies", remembering that Jesus had a band of seventy followers, in addition to the apostles, who helped Him in the work of the Kingdom. They gave us crucial help in the months before we moved into the Coach House.

Another very significant event for God's people in East Sussex took place in the autumn. Peter Ball was chosen to be Bishop of Lewes. He was consecrated Bishop in St. Paul's Cathedral on St. Luke's day and two days later was commissioned by Bishop Eric Kemp of Chichester in Holy Trinity Church, Hastings. It seemed wonderful to us that he had been appointed to this office at a time when we were emerging into public view. With his deep commitment to the religious life and community life, he later gave us great support and encouragement.

For 1978 Michael planned an ambitious programme of monthly talks at St. Peter's on the theme, 'Every Member Ministry'. Bishop Peter was the first speaker. His visit resulted in a very special evening for the Servants with Jesus. First, Bishop Peter gave a most challenging address which expanded and complemented much of our own thinking and praying for the restoration of the Church in East Sussex. Secondly, after the service the congregation retired to the Community Centre for coffee. Michael introduced Sister Eva and myself to Bishop Peter and made sure we had several minutes to speak to him on our own. He expressed much interest in the Servants with Jesus' vision and said he would like to visit us.

We invited Bishop Peter to lunch. He accepted our invitation for a day in Holy Week. His visit proved a great stimulation to our faith. After lunch we went to view the Coach House. As we went round the still derelict building he said, "Surely this is bad enough to be of God!" He was speaking from his own experience of restoring disused and ruined buildings for the glory of God. We were left with his prayers and blessing, greatly reassured and strengthened for the future.

Three contractors returned tender documents. The trustees met in February 1978 to consider their proposals. We were all agreed that Bardens of Pett were the best candidates. We had heard that they were a well-established family firm with a genuine interest in restoring old buildings. They also offered the most favourable terms, £55,556. Signing the tender documents would be a legally binding agreement which we would have to honour. It was essential that we knew we were in the centre of God's will. We were beginning to learn how important it was to discern the difference between taking steps ordained by the Lord and rushing ahead of Him.

One of the trustees felt that we should not sign the documents until we had a tenth of the total monies required in the bank. We looked at our accounts to find we were £300 short. We therefore agreed that we would meet in a week's time. Meanwhile we would pray that £300 would become available. We ourselves would not provide the money personally and we would not mention this matter to anyone. By the time we met again we had received three cheques totalling £300; so we signed the tender documents and engaged Bardens.

Early in March, Peter Evenden and Peter Barden met to fix the dates for the work. They agreed to start on 3rd April and to aim for completion by 30th November. These dates had a remarkable significance for us of which the Peters were totally unaware. 3rd April was the traditional date for celebrating the life of St. Richard of Chichester who had been so closely connected with the Manor site. Also, as things worked out after waiting over twenty years, it was the day on which work on the Old Town by-pass started. It was as though God was saying, "This is a completely new phase for the Old Town, a phase of peace and tranquillity." Before the by-pass was opened, traffic was so heavy that it was impossible to cross the road from the Manor Gardens to St. Peter's without waiting for five or more minutes. 30th November was also a significant date – St Andrew's day when the Church traditionally prays and gives thanks for missionaries. We would also be celebrating the sixth anniversary of our commissioning as Servants with Jesus. We sent an invitation to Bishop Peter asking if he would be able to dedicate the restored Coach House on that day. We were delighted that he was free to accept.

Throughout February and March our solicitor, Derek Warren, and Miss Fletcher of the Council's legal department were busy preparing the documents needed for issuing a licence for the restoration work. On 17th March we were told that it was in order for us to have vacant possession. This was perfect timing as over Easter we were able to have celebrations and prayer in the Coach House before the builders began their work.

As soon as we had the keys, Sister Eva and I swept out the old Manor servants' sitting room in the flat. It was the only room in the house where there was light, with intact windows, overlooking the grounds of East Down House. On Easter Monday we spent a day of fellowship with the Seventies, partly in our own home. In the afternoon we went to the Coach House. For some, it was their first visit. We were both awed and excited, spending time in the sitting room singing praises to God.

We then made our way through a small low doorway into the hay loft. We paused to envisage the prayer room that was to be. Douglas Noble, a wood craftsman, shared his thoughts about the need for a focal point in the place where the hoist for the hay had once been. The hoist was to be replaced with a window, stretching from ceiling to floor. A few days later he shared with us his vision of a large wooden cross, several feet high. He felt this should be placed in the window recess so that it could be seen from the Manor Gardens. He had a piece of oak in his workshop and offered to use it for this purpose. Douglas spoke with gentle yet such strong conviction that we knew he should undertake this work.

Two days later we held a Communion service in the Coach House sitting room. Michael Townroe and John Bickersteth celebrated and Edmund spoke. We borrowed chairs and prayer books from St. Peter's and took our own table, table linen and song books from Chantry Avenue. Michael and Beatrice gave us a unique gift to be used as a chalice. It was a stone goblet, commemorating the giving of the Bexhill Charter to the Christians of his day by King Offa. All the Servants, trustees and pastoral advisers were present. We met to give thanks to God for everything He had done and to pray for the protection of all who would be working on the site in the months ahead. We were blessed with a glorious sunny day which helped to fill us with anticipation and hope for the future. On 3rd April we handed over the keys of the building to Peter Barden so that the work could begin.

We had an arrangement with Bardens to send us monthly accounts to be paid within ten days. The timing of the Lord's financial provision during the following months was truly amazing. We received a steady flow of small and large gifts. I am convinced that these were released because the Servants, the Seventies and some of our prayer partners had first given themselves without reserve to the Lord for the fulfilling of His purposes. Most of them did not possess much of this world's goods but gave sacrificially as they were able.

An unusual example of this was Dorothy Baker, one of the Seventies, who later became Sister Dorothy Ellen. After church one Sunday morning she went into her garden to remove dead daffodil heads and noticed something shining on top of the soil. It was a half sovereign which must have been lying there for years. She had been asking the Lord how she could contribute to the restoration work. Here was His answer. The bank bought the coin for £30! Someone else gave us an old gramophone. We were able to sell it to two men in an antique shop for £10; they had been looking out for something that would play their old records. Over the months we received numerous gifts ranging from £1 to £500. They all helped to provide what was needed.

I was away at St. Albans visiting a friend after the first week of the building operations. Sister Eva telephoned to say that we had received an anonymous gift through the post of £1,800 via a bank manager in Kingsbridge, Devon. He said his client wished to encourage us in our work but to remain anonymous. We did not know anyone living in that area. With the monies we had already received, we were able to pay Bardens' first account at the end of April. During May, John Bickersteth telephoned to say that one of our prayer partners had given us a gift of £5,000. So by the time Bardens' May account arrived, we already had the money in hand. In June an anonymous cheque for £150 coincided with the arrival of the June account. In similar fashion, events continued throughout the year, culminating in a magnificent anonymous gift in October of £6,224 via a bank manager in Coventry!

The building team was supervised by an enthusiastic, efficient and much respected foreman, Alex Baker. He was a very special gift from God. He set up his office, with a telephone in the room that was eventually to be our office.

There were interesting discoveries and happenings during the course of the restoration work. Some were unexpected encouragements, others posed problems that had to be overcome. It was heartening to discover early on that the foundations of the building were much stronger than anticipated. Later it was a challenge to our faith when Peter Evenden told us that the whole wall to the east of the building where we had planned only to remove the chimney, would need rebuilding. Also, when work was started on the roof, the builders discovered that many of the iron pins that held the tiles in place, had rusted through. At least half of the roof would need retiling at the additional cost of £3,000.

A particularly interesting discovery was made of a small secret window when the builders were working on the south side of the roof. No such window could be seen from the inside of the building. Upon further investigation, it turned out to be a small window with a sill in the corner of the ceiling of the sitting room. It had been deliberately hidden. It looked out towards Galley Hill. Local people tell us that it was used for a lamp which gave signals to German shipping in the Great War. There were a number of German families working at the Manor in the early years of the twentieth century so this could be possible.

One of the most exciting moments for us was when all the window frames were unboarded and exposed. This happened before the end of April and after all the ivy had been stripped away. The building suddenly seemed to come to life. Another inspiring moment was in August when one evening we went to the Manor Gardens and saw that workmen had begun to paint the Coach House a sandy gold colour. In the evening sunlight it was aglow and beautiful.

A unique and exciting happening was the discovery of some Victorian copper lamps in the cellars of Ashburnham. One morning in September Sister Eva went to Communion at Penhurst Church. The Gospel for the day began with the words, "Blessed are the eyes which see the things that ye see." Luke 10:23. As she left the church, she noticed an old copper lamp at the gate of the churchyard. She asked Paul Broomhall, the churchwarden, if he knew where the lamp came from. "Yes", he said, "it is one of a dozen I bought years ago for ten shillings each in a sale at Clerkenwell. I have one lighting up my staircase and I gave several to John Bickersteth as I thought they might be useful at Ashburnham. I feel sure John would give them to you if you need them!" After breakfast at Ashburnham, John took Sister Eva to the cellars where they found three lamps of a design Peter Evenden had been looking for unsuccessfully When we showed him the lamps later in the day he was amazed.

There were two prayer battles to be fought before all the legal documentation could be agreed and signed with Rother District Council. One was about the specific area of land which should be ours and which should belong to the Parks' and Gardens' department for their rubbish dump and compost heap. The Parks' and Recreation manager, Mr. Hudson, was keen to have the area directly in front of the Coach House so that his staff would have easy access from the Manor Gardens. For our purposes, this was totally unacceptable as our main living and guest accommodation would be overlooking garden debris and grass mowings from the whole Manor site. The thought of this was offensive and seemed to us totally alien to the councillors' desire that all the restoration work should be tasteful and blend in with the environment. We suggested that the area in front of the Coach House should be included in our lease in simple exchange for the less obtrusive site to the east of the building which seemed to us much better suited to the Council's needs.

In September Sister Eva and I, Peter Evenden, Mr. Hudson and one of the solicitors from the Town Hall met on site to discuss this proposition. At first Mr. Hudson was adamant that the plans should not be changed. As the discussion continued, Peter Evenden withdrew a little and began sketching. Sister Eva also withdrew from the immediate scene so that she could pray, while I continued with the conversation. After a few minutes Peter Evenden rejoined us slightly ahead of Sister Eva. He presented us with a sketch of landscaping for the whole area. He showed it to Mr. Hudson and asked, "What do you say to this? I think this is how things should be." Mr. Hudson agreed immediately and without further questioning! This change of heart seemed to us a wonderful miracle. Some weeks later Councillor Traice 'phoned us on 17th October, late in the evening, to let us know that the Recreation and Leisure Committee had agreed to the exchange of land.

The other battle concerned the timing of our moving into the Coach House. Discussions about this began in May. Peter Evenden and the builders considered the work would be sufficiently advanced for us to move in at the beginning of November. This would give us time to get the house furnished and in order for the dedication at the end of the month. Mr. Millward, the Council's solicitor, also thought this would be possible so we started to work towards moving on 1st November. On 4th July, the Recreation and Leisure Committee agreed that we could do this. The full Council gave their seal of approval to our plan at their meeting at the end of the month. They also authorised their architect to put in hand immediately remedial work that was needed on a section of the main sewer from the Coach House, work which was their responsibility. However on 25th October, Douglas Chamberlain discovered that the drain had not been repaired.

Sister Eva and I had arranged with Alex that furniture in store should be moved into the Coach House on 31st October and that our own furniture from Chantry Avenue should be moved on 3rd November. On 30th October I telephoned Mr. Mead, the chief administrative officer at the Town Hall, to tell him our plans and he gave his blessing to the arrangements we had made. I went early to the Coach House on 1st November to see how the inside decorating was progressing. I met an anxious Alex who shared with me the urgency of the water situation. He said that Bardens could do the work themselves but they must have the Council's approval. Peter Evenden went quickly to work and got the necessary permission. He also got into touch with the Waterboard about meters.

On 3rd November, the day for moving to our "Jerusalem" arrived. It was a beautiful sunny day which made the work pleasant. The Sisters and Seventies rallied to give much practical help as Sister Eva and I moved on to the top floor of the Coach House. One of the Seventies brought us a delicious lunch. Sister Dorothy Mary made our beds, which was greatly appreciated for by the end of the day we were exhausted.

The climax of the move was in the evening when Douglas Noble brought the cross he had made and placed it in the prayer room. Sister Eva and I had seen it a few days before. When Sister Eva first saw the cross, she was speechless. It was the one she had seen in August 1970 at an East Sussex prayer meeting with the words "Stat Crux Dum Volvitur Orbis"! Douglas knew nothing of this vision.

The following day, at the end of our first full day at the Coach House, Michael and Beatrice Townroe joined some of the Servants and Seventies in the prayer room. Michael led us in Compline and asked God's blessing on us all for the future.

The Prayer Room, converted from the old Manor hayloft with the Cross carved by Douglas Noble.

Chapter Fifteen

Taking our Stand in Jerusalem

"I was glad when they said to me, 'Let us go to the house of the Lord!' Our feet have been standing within your gates, O Jerusalem." Psalm 122:1-2

"Jerusalem it shall be! I think the name has a prophetic content. We do not fully understand the significance at present but the meaning will unfold."

These were the words of Bishop Peter when Sister Eva and I visited him the previous August to talk about the dedication and naming of the Coach House.

Over the years, the Servants with Jesus were unanimous in referring to the Coach House as Jerusalem and had decided that the address on our new headed note paper would begin with Jerusalem. Michael Townroe, interestingly, challenged our decision. He was concerned that the inner meaning of the word 'Jerusalem' should not be diminished. For him, Jerusalem was a warm, positive scriptural concept. Wherever people met in Christ, there was the new Jerusalem. He wanted to be sure that the flow of the Biblical imagery would not be lost. He did not want there to be any possibility of people thinking the Servants were being over-the-top!

Bishop Peter picked up some hesitation on our part when we spoke about the name 'Jerusalem'. "Aren't the Sisters agreed?" he asked. "Yes" we replied. We then explained the difficulties. Bishop Peter paused for a minute or so and gave his very positive response. Michael, assured that we understood the implications of our decision, gave his full support and encouragement to our plans.

There were barely four weeks to get our Jerusalem and ourselves ready for the dedication. There was much hard work to be done. Our accommodation for the first few days might be described as good indoor camping conditions.

We were living on the top floor as the flat still needed decorating. There was no running water. On the ground floor, there was plastic sheeting where the windows should have been so locking the doors at night provided no security. We set up a temporary living room in the main bedroom. We armed ourselves with several large plastic containers for water. For washing and toilets, we used the facilities provided for visitors to the Manor Gardens. We visited these each day at about 6.30 am, taking the dog with us, we collected water for the day. We felt it important to achieve all this before the gardeners and builders arrived to start the day's work. This routine was repeated in the evening before retiring for the night.

For the first two weeks in November, we were blessed with unusually fine weather for the time of year. This was a great help as there were many matters which needed attention.

We visited the lighting centres in Bexhill and Hastings to choose lights and fittings for the whole house. We found twelve matching amber glass lampshades for the two public rooms. This was a very good discovery, ideal for our purpose. We were told that the lamps were an unusual assignment from Poland. We thought they would be right to create an atmosphere of warmth in rooms that faced north and were dull and gloomy in cloudy weather.

We collected spare carpeting from friends who were recarpeting their own homes. We were fortunate in having the help of a young Christian engineer who was working on the new by-pass. Pete was living in a caravan on the work site. The first week we were in residence, he spent the evenings with us fitting carpet in all the top floor rooms. This was an immense task, especially as there was not a single straight wall or floor in the building. We cooked Pete an evening meal and enjoyed fellowship together. He was a real gift from God, blessed with tremendous energy and physical strength.

We were also busy during this first week cleaning and clearing up at Chantry Avenue, as the sale was not yet completed. We had numerous bonfires. We had left some of our furniture in the house until the flat in Jerusalem was ready. This meant too that we had a place of retreat when we needed a break from all the noise and bustle of building activities.

It was a great relief when four days after our arrival at the Coach House, the water was turned on, for the top floor. On the fifth day a digger arrived to start work on the drains. By the end of the day the main drain pipes were in place.

On the sixth day we went to Chantry Avenue at about nine o'clock in the morning. There was a letter waiting for us from our solicitor saying, "'Phone me as soon as possible!" We had to return to the Coach House as the telephone was disconnected. I asked Alex if I could use the telephone in his office. I had anticipated that he would leave the room but he stayed and continued to work quietly.

I telephoned Derek Warren in London. "Where are you?" he asked. "In the Coach House," I replied. "Good! he said, "I am pleased to know that you have not been evicted!" This was an astonishing remark. He had received a letter from a member of the solicitors' department at the Town Hall. It was a different solicitor from the two with whom we had already been negotiating. He instructed our solicitor to tell us that we were not to move into the Coach House on 1st November as the drains were not in place and our flat was not ready for occupation.

In the providence of God, this letter had been sent to our solicitor in London, rather than directly to us in Chantry Avenue. Derek Warren was away on holiday when it arrived so it remained unanswered and, in blissful ignorance, we moved into the Coach House. When Derek Warren read the letter he had tried telephoning us unsuccessfully! He had to write to us instead, causing yet further delay. I was able to tell him that work had begun on the drains and the decoration of the flat. We agreed I would get in touch with him at the end of the day to report on progress, before he answered the letter.

Alex had listened to the conversation and picked up the urgency of the situation. "Disappear for the day!" he said. "Don't let me know where you are going. Should anyone turn up to see you, you will not be here to be evicted! Come back at the time we finish work! I will let you know of any developments."

We followed this advice and when we returned later, we found that Alex had deployed all his work force to deal with the two main problems. He told us that the drains had been connected and were in working order. His men had been working on the flat and it would be ready for occupation by the weekend. This seemed to us a miracle as it was Thursday and there was only one more working day.

While we had been absent from the Coach House, the Lord had spoken to us through a scripture promise. It was the command of Moses to the Israelites at the Red Sea, as the Egyptian armies approached: "Stand firm and see the salvation of the Lord, which He will work for you today." Exodus 14:13. It seemed the Lord was already working for us. Late in the afternoon, I telephoned Derek Warren to report on the current situation.

We knew that on the following Monday evening, a full Council meeting was planned. Sister Eva and I thought it important that a reply should be made to the Council's solicitor to arrive on his desk on Monday morning. The letter should explain that we had moved into the Coach House with the permission of the Chief Administrative Officer, having no knowledge of his letter. The drains were already in order and the flat would be ready to move into over the weekend. He hoped therefore that his clients would be allowed to remain in residence.

Derek Warren considered this to be a good strategy and arranged for his secretary to get a letter into the Friday afternoon post.

That same afternoon, we were relaxing in our top floor sitting room when two Christian friends unexpectedly arrived – Oliver Styles of the Scripture Union who was conducting a children's mission in the area and Edwin Purse, Minister of the Welcome Mission at Heathfield. Not knowing our predicament, they had come with a scripture: "When the enemy shall come in like a flood, the Spirit of the Lord shall lift up a standard against him." Isaiah 59:19. While they were still with us, Peter Evenden arrived to see how work was progressing. He had come straight from a luncheon for the Grammar School governors where, as chairman, he sat next to Bishop Peter, the guest of honour. "The Sisters are in trouble," he said, "They have been told to leave the Coach House." "I can't see those two moving out!" was Bishop Peter's response. It was most reassuring to have episcopal blessing to dig in our heels and stay put.

On Saturday Douglas Noble helped us lay carpets in the flat and put furniture in place. If Council officials arrived on Monday, we wanted them to see the flat fully operational. Council officials did in fact turn up on Monday morning while we were out. Alex showed them over the house and flat and gave details about the state of the drains. In the evening Douglas attended the Council meeting and heard their recommendation that we should stay in residence.

The following morning, the last items of furniture were removed from Chantry Avenue into the flat. By the evening, there was a storm and heavy rain. Stormy weather continued for several days. The fine weather had lasted until everything was aboard, so to speak, and we were able to batten down the hatches!

There was a fortnight left to put the finishing touches to the first and second floors of our new home before the dedication. The ground floor would not be ready for use, so the flat would have to be used for hospitality after the dedication of the house and time of worship in the prayer room.

Our sixth anniversary on St. Andrew's day was a wonderful climax to a year of God's leading and provision. Early in the evening, Bishop Peter read Psalm 122 at the side door and named the Coach House 'Jerusalem'. The assembled company of about thirty-five then followed him round the house as he prayed in each room and asked for God's blessing. It was essentially a family occasion with the Servants and their husbands, the trustees, pastoral advisers and their wives, the Seventies and Peter Evenden and his wife. We all managed to fit into the prayer room for the Communion service. This was a glorious service of thanksgiving and dedication. Bishop Peter blessed some of the wooden crosses that Terrell had brought us from Jerusalem and gave one to each of the Seventies who were committing themselves to serve at our Jerusalem, with prayer and practical help.

For the ministry of the word, Bishop Peter spoke about the wonder of being called to be with Jesus in prayer and suffering so that we could be sent out by Him to love and serve others. John Bickersteth brought us a word of promise from the scriptures, convinced that the witness to the risen Jesus would go far beyond the Coach House: "You shall receive power when the Holy Spirit has come upon you; and you shall be My witnesses in Jerusalem, and in all Judea and Samaria and to the end of the earth." Acts 1:8.

The Eucharist that November evening was a time of exceeding great joy, awe and wonder in the presence of the risen Lord. We marvelled at all He had done for us. The most moving thing for me was the depth of the Lord's gift of unity we experienced as we worshipped together. He was indeed doing great things for us and we were glad!

Above: Christmas in the 1960's with my parents and brother Selwyn. *Bottom left:* St Peter's flower festival, 29th June 1972 – depicting King Offa with the Bexhill Charter 722 AD. *Bottom right:* Michael and Beatice Townroe at home.

The Coach House April 1978.

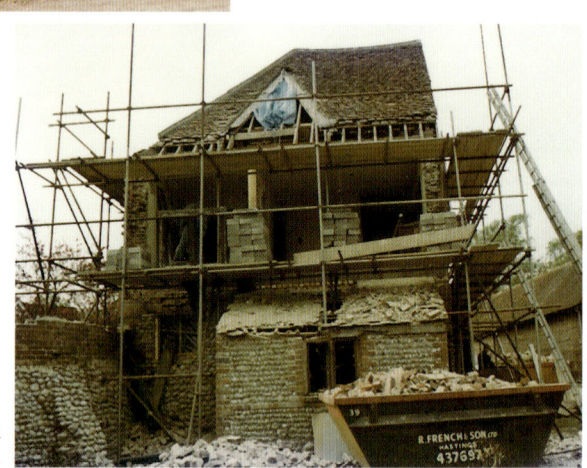

Right and below: Restoration work in progress, summer 1978.

Claiming the Promised Land in the Coach House yard – Sister Eva Lowe, Sister Dorothy Mary Osborn and Sister Dorothy MacGill.

The Coach House July 1979.

Our first winter in Jerusalem – December 1978.

View from the Prayer Room Window. *Above:* June 1979. *Below:* Summer 1980

Christmas at the Jerusalem Hospice. *Top left:* Sister Dorothy Ellen Sharp (neé Baker) carving the turkey. *Top right:* Christmas lunch. *Bottom left:* Sister Eva sorting out the Christmas presents. *Bottom right:* A patient with a Jerusalem helper.

Bishop Peter with the first schemers – Anne, Katrina and Jeannie.

John Bickersteth with the Ashburnham P.C.C. for an away day at Jerusalem.

The Servants with Jesus family relaxing and celebrating in Jerusalem

Top left: Douglas Noble, Sister Rene Noble and Sister Eileen Wheeler. *Top right:* Sister Sylvia McEniry.
Below: Bishop Peter with Sister Marjorie Rowson, Sister Anne Witchell and Sister Anna Emmens.

Bottom left: Sister Edna Cole, Sister Gillian Wootten, Ken Wootten and George Cole.
Bottom right: Sister Janet Bradshaw, Dennis Nolan, John Osborn and Sister Jean Luke Plouviez.

Above: The Servants taking a break for two away days at Ashburnham Prayer Centre, April 1993.
Below: With may brother Selwyn after ordination on the 9th July 1995.

Above: Celebrating at Jerusalem, 10th July 1995.

Sister Gillian Wootten with one of her flower arrangements.

Sister Gillian Wootten preparing for a full meeting of the Servants.

The wilderness to the South East of Jerusalem, before the Prayer Garden was created.

Approach to the Prayer Garden.

The fountain in the Prayer Garden.

28th June 1999 – after the blessing of the Prayer Garden by Bishop Wallace Benn.
Photo: Bexhill Observer

Jerusalem as seen today from the walled garden in the Manor Gardens.

Chapter Sixteen

Living in Jerusalem

"Be glad and rejoice .... in that which I create .... Jerusalem a rejoicing and her people a joy." Isaiah 65:18

".... it was a great, great evening and I rejoice with you, with exceedingly great joy. The Lord has blessed you .... I am certain that there is much that we can do together and that is my privilege. O Jerusalem, my happy home!"

I was deeply moved and humbled by a letter we received from Bishop Peter a few days after the dedication of the Coach House, expressing these sentiments.

We were about to experience the reality of living the Jerusalem life. It was full of surprises. We had to learn to live one day at a time, to respond to each circumstance as it arose. A second priority was to be available to God's people. By sending them to us, the Lord was creating His New Jerusalem amongst us. In our corporate life in our earthly Jerusalem, we were at times to catch a glimpse of God's New Jerusalem in heaven and on earth. Worship and prayer were at the centre of our daily lives. When that was so, the joy, peace and love of God's Spirit flowed amongst us, achieving His creative work.

Early in the new year, a pattern for our corporate prayer life unfolded. This was while Sister Eva and I were enjoying two God-given weeks, resting in Jerusalem. These were much needed after the intense activity of the past year. There were several heavy snow falls. The paths and roads were icy and dangerous. Very few people braved the elements to make their way to Jerusalem. We were able to put to the test our new Yorkstone fireplace and restored chimney, while relaxing in the warmth of coal and log fires.

A weekly plan for our corporate prayer life began to emerge. First, the cross in the prayer room inspired us to set aside three hours every Friday to pray from noon to three o'clock. This became a time of intercessory prayer for East Sussex. Although the Servants and Seventies were free to come and go during that period, we sought between us to maintain continuous prayer. In particular, we concentrated on praying for Christian leaders and the proclamation of the Gospel for the coming weekend.

Secondly, we were shown that on weekday mornings we should pray for half an hour at ten o'clock before the house was opened to the public.

Our third commitment was to meet on Thursday evenings with the local Servants with Jesus and Seventies. These times were to become significant meetings for worship, reading the scriptures and seeking God's will in prayer.

Our monthly meetings with all the Servants were still to be a major priority. They continued to be the main context for hearing God's word, receiving guidance and making decisions.

Central to our daily living was trusting the Lord to provide for all the human and material resources needed. There was still the restoration on the ground floor to be completed. Outside the old stableyard needed landscaping and turning into a garden that would blend with the surroundings. Provision was also needed to give decent and relaxing hospitality to all who came.

The Lord continued to provide in remarkable and precise ways. For example, two of our prayer partners came to have coffee with us one morning. As they said, "Goodbye", they left us a gift of £100. When we opened

The Reading Room at the Coach House before and after restoration.

an envelope that had been put through the letter box, while we had been enjoying our time together, it was the electricity bill!

Another lovely incident of God's caring concerned our adorable and mischievous longhaired dachshund. His vet told us that it was essential he should have major surgery if we were to keep him. During the week of his operation, we were given two generous personal gifts which met the cost. He lived to be seventeen years of age!

During our early Jerusalem days, we were challenged and tested about our life style of faith. We knew that before the summer was over, there would be a number of large bills to pay in connection with the landscaping and final work on the house. Sister Eva and I became increasingly convinced that we should sell our new car as a contribution towards the costs. A few months before moving into the Coach House, we had both sold our ageing cars and bought one new car between us so that we would have reliable transport for all that was involved in the move. Our new car was still in its first year and we knew we would be likely to get a good price.

Our trustees were at first very discouraging about this proposition, out of concern for our well-being. At a trustees' meeting in May, we had a full discussion about our financial principles. Sister Eva and I were convinced that the future basis on which we should operate should be very much like that of George Muller. From the time I left the Grammar School, I had attempted to live in the same way. God had honoured this practice. George Muller's story had inspired me greatly. The way God provided for all the children in his homes, without advertising the needs, had always filled me with wonder. By the end of the meeting, the trustees agreed that this should be our future practice. We would not make a set charge for guests but accept donations. They also concluded that God was leading us in the matter of selling the car.

Our trustees need not have been anxious on our behalf. It was a part of God's plan for us to be without a car for a time. Having no car relieved us of numerous current commitments. With a car still in our possession, it would have been difficult to extricate ourselves without hurting others. We came to realise there would have been no point in the Lord sending people to us in our Jerusalem, if we were out and about in East Sussex.

We received our last large account from Bardens at the end of June. The sale of the car would make a good contribution towards this but there was a shortfall of several thousand pounds. Our trustee, Douglas Chamberlain, would need to add his signature to the cheque for payment. He had moved to Oxford so Sister Eva sent him a cheque for the appropriate amount for signing.

John Bickersteth had been away for several days and on his return telephoned. Sister Eva answered the 'phone. "What are you doing about the payment of Bardens' account due tomorrow?" he asked. "We have sent Douglas a cheque to sign", she replied, "and we are expecting it to be returned by tomorrow's post." "Is there money in the account to meet the payment?" he continued. "Not at the moment", Sister Eva responded, "but we expect the -Lord will have provided by tomorrow". "Are you certain about that?" John pressed. "Yes, absolutely!" returned Sister Eva. "You are absolutely right", he said, "when I returned to Ashburnham there was a cheque waiting for you for £7,500. It is an anonymous gift from a lady who has recovered from a serious illness. She has heard of your work and wants to give thanks to God by sending you this donation!"

In addition to amazing financial gifts, we received several unique and special gifts in kind.

One day in May, Will Perrin and his wife, Ida, arrived at the Coach House. I had met them on a number of previous occasions through my close friends, Will and Vi Sidnell. They had come to find out how we were getting on. While they were with us, Will, who enjoyed painting and sketching, made a generous suggestion. He offered to produce a greetings notelet with pen and ink sketches of the Coach House at his own expense. We readily accepted. The notelet was popular with visitors and used to spread the news around of the peace and refreshment that could be found at Jerusalem.

In June we received a special personal gift for our flat kitchen. Two of our Seventies had noticed that our electric cooker had reached its sell-by-date and sacrificially, I believe, provided us with a new one.

Another unusual gift was released to us by Colin Hudson of the Parks and Gardens Department. In March, Bardens had engaged someone with a large mechanical digger to begin landscaping the whole of our garden area. The soil exposed was of poor quality and full of cobbles as the ground had originally formed the surface of the manor stableyard. Several inches of good top soil were needed if we were to have a healthy lawn and flourishing plants and shrubs. Peter Evenden and Peter Barden had unsuccessfully explored a number of possibilities. One day Councillor Traice visited us. When we shared our predicament, she said that there was an enormous pile of very good top soil in the grounds of St. Jude's at Barrack Hall, only a few hundred yards away from us. She would speak to Colin Hudson and ask him if it could be released for our use. He not only agreed but arranged for the soil to be delivered.

A few weeks later in the middle of June, Mr. Luck and his sons, experienced landscape gardeners, arrived to prepare the soil for laying the lawn. Some friends had expressed concern that we were attempting to lay turfs in June. "They will never take!" seemed to be the general opinion. We were very relieved when Mr. Luck arrived to hear him say, "This is the best day there has been so far this year for laying turf!" And so it proved to be. Within two days the lawn was laid. Mr Luck's sons came to water the lawn regularly; the turfs settled and integrated quickly and within a very short time we had a beautiful lawn.

Friends brought us all manner of plants for the flower borders. Colin Hudson recommended a number of suitable shrubs which we were able to purchase and plant at the weekend. It had taken only a week to transform a barren yard into a pleasant garden.

God's continuing provision and the perfect timing and interweaving of so many events was a constant source of wonder. Still more amazing was the great variety of individuals and groups the Lord sent to us. We found ourselves giving hospitality to people from widely different Christian traditions and social backgrounds. The Holy Spirit drew us close to them all in fellowship and understanding. We experienced, in cameo, something of the life of the New Jerusalem. We enjoyed remarkable unity in the Spirit.

It became more and more evident that true Spirit-inspired unity in the whole Church was a crucial element in preparation for Revival. Thoughts from Psalm 133 were important to us as step by step we became a catalyst for the unity of God's people: "Behold, how good and pleasant it is when brothers dwell in unity! .... there the Lord has commanded the blessing, life for evermore." It is perhaps not surprising that over the years our unity has been viciously attacked.

During our early years at the Coach House, we revelled in new friendships and relationships. Some groups came to hear our story; others came to stay for a few days to pray and seek the Lord. We were often rewarded with encouragement from our visitors.

It was hard work catering for our guests and preparing rooms for those who stayed overnight. The Seventies were magnificent in all the practical help and support they gave, sometimes noticing what needed to be done before we asked.

Our first visitors were a group of young people from the Welcome Mission at Heathfield. Their young assistant minister, Steve Brading, called early one afternoon in February to ask if they could come to hear our story. He wanted them to learn how to pray and claim God's promises. If they could actually see over the house, he thought the wonder of all God had done, would make a strong impression.

"We have no furniture yet in the main meeting room", we explained. "There is carpeting. If you don't mind sitting on the floor, we would love to have you!" They came. Their visit was a highlight for us. The evening finished with a moving time of thanksgiving and prayer when everyone spontaneously fell to their knees.

Our contact with Steve was special. This was truly a God-given appointment. Steve looked so tired that first afternoon he called to see us that Sister Eva invited him to rest in our sitting room and join us for a meal later. He readily accepted and fell asleep on our sofa. An hour or so later, two young women appeared at our gate. One was Ruth Anderson, the daughter of Jock and Gwendy Anderson, who had been friends of mine at university. I had not seen Ruth since she was a child. Gwendy had suggested that she called to see how we were while she was staying with a friend in Bexhill.

I was showing Ruth and her friend round the house when Sister Eva remembered that Steve was asleep in the sitting room. It would be only a matter of minutes before we entered the room. She woke Steve just in time to greet the ladies. Steve and Ruth saw each other for barely ten minutes. For Steve it was a case of love at first sight! By August, they were engaged to be married. Other visits from church groups followed – first another young peoples' group from a Baptist church. A local Anglican group came for a quiet day. We welcomed evening groups from Anglican and Brethren congregations. They came to hear our story which we usually illustrated with slides. One evening while we were doing this, I heard someone in the first row saying, "Isn't it wonderful? It's like a fairy story!" This was hardly the impression we intended to give! However, the remark does give some idea of the strong effect made by the telling of God's wonderful works.

We welcomed numbers of women's fellowships, including groups from a United Reformed church, several Baptist churches and several parish churches. One lady was heard to say, "This is the Lord's doing and it is marvellous in our eyes!"

Two groups of church elders came to stay for several days, one from Durrington Baptist church, the other from Emsworth Community church. We were greatly encouraged that they felt God had spoken to them during their visits. Ashburnham PCC was the first of a number of PCCs who came to us for away days

Two memorable occasions were a Saturday visit from the Emsworth Community church and a visit of Bishop Peter's prayer partners to tea.

Ian McCulloch and his wife, Sister Phyllis, arrived one Saturday morning with about eighty members of their Emsworth congregation. They wanted their people to hear how God had led us and provided! Their enthusiastic response to the things we shared, strengthened our own faith. In the afternoon, they had a time of praise and worship which could be heard all over the Manor Gardens. The volume of praise rivalled that of contemporary Saturday night discos in the Manor Barn. The difference was that whatever the neighbours thought, we received no complaints.

Bishop Peter brought about one hundred and twenty prayer partners to the Coach House one afternoon towards the end of July. Their visit coincided with completion of work on the driveway and garden. It was a time of exceptional joy. The Spirit poured out a supernatural joy which we all recognised. The next day, Bishop Peter wrote to us saying, "Never have I felt so filled with joy as when I walked into your home yesterday and saw all those saints of God .... It was thrilling beyond words ...."

On the same day one of Sir Lester and Lady Harmsworth's daughters telephoned us. She had been present at the tea party. Her parents were the last private owners of the Manor. She asked if she and her sister could visit us on Sunday afternoon. They were thrilled with all the restoration work. They shared how both their parents were Christians and would have been so happy to know how the Coach House was being used. It was an unusually interesting afternoon. We walked round the Manor House ruins and they told us how the different rooms had been used.

We also received visits from servants who had lived in the Coach House. When Ivy Groves, who had been Lady Harmsworth's personal maid, visited us she was moved to tears. She had been very sad to see the Coach House decaying and falling apart and was overwhelmed when she saw the restoration work. She was a member of the Salvation Army and was really excited that her old home was now a place for prayer and Christian ministry.

Two other aspects of ministry developed during these early days. One was contact with the local community, the other was hospitality to Christian workers, especially those working overseas who needed rest and refreshment.

Some councillors and members of Rother District staff visited us from time to time. They came to see how we were getting on and sometimes to ask for prayer. One of them shared how he recognised God's hand was upon us.

Mr. Dudman of the Planning Department was a great encouragement. He was so pleased with the restoration work on the Coach House that he suggested we entered a civic building contest.

Members of the Old Town Preservation Society asked us many questions so we invited them for coffee and to see the slides. The local Townswomen's Guild also came for an evening. When all the restoration work was completed, we invited Bardens' men and their wives to coffee. We showed them the slides. They were amazed when we shared with them how God had provided the money to pay their accounts. We were touched by a gift they brought of two albums of photographs. These formed an excellent record of their discoveries and activities during the demolition and rebuilding work.

Our main contact with the public came through opening the gates into the Manor Gardens. These were opened each weekday from 10.30 am to the end of the afternoon. Servants or Seventies were on duty to greet everyone who came. On fine days there would be twenty to thirty people visiting us. Some came out of curiosity to see the building; others came because they were lonely and wanted to talk; some came asking for prayer. From time to time small groups of holiday makers from the Granville Hotel made their way to us for morning coffee.

On bank holidays, we opened for the whole day. One afternoon a lady arrived and after chatting with a number of people, approached me asking, "Everyone here knows God, don't they?" It seemed she herself was wanting to know God. I suggested we went to the prayer room to talk. I gave her one of our cards which spoke about Jesus being "the way, the truth and the life". I explained what this meant and we prayed together before she left.

One day Councillor Traice arrived with her friend, Elsie Eames. Elsie had brought with her a very special gift. For the Charter celebration year, she and a friend had made a collection of dolls, dressed in the style of 772 AD, for exhibition in the De La Warr Pavilion. These depicted King Offa with his royal household giving the Bexhill Charter to Bishop Oswald and his monks. A group of Saxon villagers were in the background. We display these dolls in our refreshment area. They are often a talking point, especially for children who enjoy looking at them, while they listen to the story of Bexhill's Christian beginnings.

People with all kinds of needs came through our gates. It was wonderful to see how the Lord stage-managed everything. So often the person on duty had experienced the same problem and so was able to listen with understanding.

House guests who came from abroad usually stayed between one to three weeks. Fellowship with them was mutually enriching and rewarding.

Amongst our guests were Terrell and Laura Boyes. They worked at the Garden Tomb in Jerusalem. We learnt many things from them about the original earthly Jerusalem which gave us insights about the spiritual life of the New Jerusalem. This special bond led to us distributing their prayer letter and sometimes, gathering their local prayer partners together.

Pennie Thomson, a nurse from Nepal, came to convalesce. We have kept in touch with her over the years. She is now Pennie Woodcraft and with her husband, Peter, leads the prayer ministry in the prayer centre at Ashburnham. Other regular guests were Ruth Sutter and Esther Muller, two young women from Switzerland. Ruth was attracted to our way of life and came to test if she had a call to be a Servant with Jesus. She was eventually led with two others to start a small community for single women in Basle. In 1998, I had the great joy and privilege of visiting them for a few days. They lead a disciplined prayer life and welcome numerous guests. Their home is a centre of peace and refuge for those living in a busy city. As a Servant with Jesus, I felt very much at home.

Living in our Jerusalem proved to be exceptionally demanding. We never knew what was waiting for us round the corner or where the human resources would come from to cope with the next situation.

The Spirit sometimes led Dr. Denis Ball to stay with us when he was in the area. His visits were always opportune – just when we were needing a word of direction or encouragement. One such occasion was in April 1980. As we were praying together he spoke a prophetic word. This helped us to look positively into a challenging Jerusalem future:

"Lift up your eyes! The fields are already ripe for harvest. When you ask Me to send out labourers into the harvest, do not be surprised at those I send. I will send the weak and lonely. I will send them to be anointed and commissioned. Look with the Spirit's eye …. this one and that one will be chosen. Their ministry will be gentle. They will be changed and renewed. They will be a kingdom – a mirror kingdom, to be a reflection of the greater Kingdom – living and sharing together for all around to see …. This will be a place of sanctuary, of refuge, a city of refuge …. Be glad and rejoice and be found strong in the Lord your God."

Chapter Seventeen

God's Workers

"God chose what is weak in the world to shame the strong .... so that no human being might boast ...." I Corinthians 1:27-29

The 'labourers' who came during the next three to four years were a delightful mixture. Some were indeed weak, broken and lonely but viewed with the Spirit's eye, each had special gifts to offer. Others had valuable expertise which contributed towards the smooth running of our Jerusalem life and household. Some lived with us for short periods of time; others for months or years. Some were young, full of energy, often impetuous; others were mature in years, bringing with them a variety of wisdom and experience.

God Himself brought us all together. The Spirit helped us to live and enjoy His abundant life. We were able to encourage and support one another.

Our first new Jerusalem family members were three of Bishop Peter's Schemers as they came to be known. They were young people who had responded to his, "Give a Year to God!" scheme. Bishop Peter's vision was for the young to share in community life for a few weeks and then to go out and bring joy to the parishes of East Sussex. For their training weeks, the boys lived at Litlington with Bishop Peter's community and the girls with us at the Coach House.

In July 1980, the first girls arrived to share our Jerusalem life – Katrina, Jeannie and Anne. We shared life together for ten demanding and exciting weeks. Katrina had recently left school, Jeannie had just completed a degree course at university and Anne had been earning her living. It was a very real challenge to each one of us. We were all so different. Bishop Peter was keen for the girls to live humbly and simply. He wanted them to be taught three things – the Gospel, how to pray and how to live together. His prime consideration was for them to share in a corporate life, not just a community life. Our priority therefore was to be worship at the Lord's table, sharing the same Bread.

Our daily routine began with Communion at St. Peter's. This was followed by breakfast together and a full morning of practical work. Assignments included all manner of activities such as preparing meals, shopping, housework, gardening, looking after visitors and visiting the sick.

After lunch there was a short break for relaxation and then teaching and discussion sessions, sometimes led by invited speakers. We all attended Evensong at St. Peter's. After supper, we enjoyed a family leisure time in the sitting room, reading, sewing, knitting and talking about many and varied topics. We shared Compline together at 8.30 pm in the prayer room after which we were all ready for bed!

Our first somewhat difficult task was getting Katrina, Jeannie and Anne clothed in the right attire. Bishop Peter wanted the Schemers to wear a common distinctive dress, something that would say, "We belong to each other". He felt it was important that they could be easily identified as belonging to the scheme. He had in mind navy fishermen's smocks with a large red cross sewn on to the front of each garment.

Sister Eva and I had been unsuccessful in finding suitable readymade smocks. We did however find some very nice soft navy denim in an Eastbourne shop. We purchased a stock of this material and some red felt. The day after their arrival, the girls set to work, under Sister Eva's supervision, to make their new clothes. They were all hard at work when Bishop Peter called to see how they were getting on. I think he was quite impressed by their skill. Jeannie was particularly adept and helped the others to produce very wearable smocks within four days. They were invited to take Evensong at St. Peter's the next day, wearing their special distinctive garments. This was their initiation into a corporate ministry

The girls gave the Servants and Seventies much joy. It was very strenuous sharing with them their full discipline of life and trying to help them to relate to each other. They brought with them though a breath of fresh air and great hope for the future. We admired their courage as they went visiting, shopping and walking about in Bexhill in their unique clothes. This provided a talking point and they were asked many questions.

At the beginning of September, we invited Father Stanley Cann of All Saints' Sidley to supper to meet the girls. This was with a view to them serving in and seeking to bring joy to his parish. Father Stanley gave an enthusiastic welcome and invited them to help with the young adventurers' club. Katrina and Jeannie moved into a bungalow in the parish later in the month.

So that they could pay for their rent and living expenses, Katrina found work as a nursing auxiliary in the Normanhurst nursing home and Jeannie as a cashier in Boots.

Two days before they left us, Bishop Peter came to commission Katrina and Jeannie and to confirm Katrina. Brother Hugh accompanied him with a loving gift from the brothers in his community towards their housekeeping. Katrina's and Jeannie's families and Father Stanley joined us for this service of simple blessing in our prayer room. Everything that took place was truly beautiful with a tremendous awareness of the outpouring of the Holy Spirit.

Throughout the Schemers' time with us, we had kept to our regular pattern of worship and prayer with the Servants and the Seventies. Our times of meeting on Thursday evenings were often in the context of a Communion service. We invited church leaders from different traditions to preside on these occasions.

The Seventies and those Servants who served at the Coach House grew closer and closer over the months. The family team was much strengthened when Mary Sherratt, a retired missionary nursing sister from the Rwanda Mission joined the Seventies. She brought with her a wealth of experience and pastoral understanding.

Douglas and Rene Noble continued to give us valiant support. Whenever Sister Eva and I were away on holiday or visiting our families, they manned Jerusalem and looked after all those who visited the house.

It was a great sadness to us all when we learnt in October that Lily Hall, one of the Seventies and our 'chocolate cake' friend, had terminal cancer. She was over eighty and had been living on her own. She came to live with us in Jerusalem, rather than going into a nursing home. Her doctor was happy for her to be with us as Sister Eva was a nurse by profession. For me, it was a new experience to live with someone who was on the last stage of their earthly journey. Being with Lily, lifted us into a new dimension. The veil between heaven and earth seemed very thin.

Lily lived with us for nearly three months. We spent Christmas together as she grew weaker. Looking after Lily required much from us physically, emotionally and spiritually. Yet she herself, being what she was, made a very special contribution to our Jerusalem life. Also her presence drew numerous people to the house. Her doctor came every few days. Community and Macmillan nurses called regularly. Many members of Beulah Baptist church visited, both young and old. Lily had been a wonderful 'mother in Israel' over the years. Those who knew her were eager to show their appreciation and to have fellowship with her again before the time came for saying, "Goodbye!" Neville Barnett, her minister, visited often to encourage Lily and to pray with her.

Lily, who had led such an active life serving others, did not find it easy to have others waiting on her. She was able though to face the prospect of death courageously and with reality. She wanted to distribute some of her most precious possessions to family and friends personally, while she was still alive. She would ask us to collect specific things from her flat and then invite a relative or friend to visit her. She would say, "Goodbye!" to them and then give them a carefully selected present. One memorable visit was from a great nephew and his fiancee, who were soon to be married. She sent for them to come for the day and gave them a much treasured tea service.

The most moving event for me during Lily's stay was during one early evening just before Christmas. Sister Eva, Lily and I were in our sitting, room, which in those days overlooked the grounds of East Down House. We heard carols being sung very close at hand. We looked out of the window. Beneath a winter flowering tree, full of light pink blossom, were about thirty members of Beulah, with lights and carol sheets. They had come to sing to Lily. We helped her to the window where she was able to stand for a few minutes and watch and listen. She waved to them all. For most of them that was the last time they saw Lily on this earth.

Lily died early in the new year. Her funeral at Beulah was well attended considering the number of Lily's contemporaries who had already gone to be with the Lord. It was a wonderful service of thanksgiving for her life.

The trustees' meeting the previous October started with a time of prayer in the prayer room. As we prayed, John Bickersteth sensed that there was going to be a new departure for us which we were to accept joyfully. He did not know what this would be but he was convinced that something new was about to break through.

At the time, we too had no idea of what this could mean. We were soon to discover that Lily's time with us was the seed of a vision, showing that we were to open a small hospice in Bexhill. In due course, the fulfilling of this vision enlarged the boundaries of our Jerusalem family far beyond our previous thoughts. Helpers joined us from outside East Sussex; some came from different parts of the United Kingdom; others from distant nations.

Chapter Eighteen

Hospice Preparations

"I say to you, unless a grain of wheat falls into the earth and dies, it remains alone, but if it dies, it bears much fruit." John 12:24

The telephone rang. It was the sister on duty from Bexhill Hospital to tell us that Lily had just died peacefully.

Sister Eva and I were in the middle of composing a letter to Dr. Victor Vaughan of St. Leonards. This was our first step towards discovering if we should be opening a hospice in Bexhill. The timing of the call was no coincidence but rather a confirmation of our recent thinking.

Two weeks earlier we had relinquished caring for Lily. We no longer had the strength required to look after her. We regretted this deeply. I shall never forget the pain of parting as the ambulance men carried her downstairs to take her to hospital.

Soon after Lily's death, Neville Barnett came to lead a Communion service in our prayer room for the Servants and Seventies. As we had all gathered some time before his arrival, Sister Eva and I shared our conviction that we should be thinking about establishing a hospice in Bexhill. There was a warm, positive response. Everyone had helped to care for Lily and, like us, were all very sad that she had to go to hospital. It did not seem the right moment to tell Neville our thoughts when he arrived. He spoke during the service from ICorinthians 15:58 – the words which had released us in 1972 to move forward: "Therefore, my beloved brethren be steadfast, immovable, always abounding in the work of the Lord, knowing that in the Lord your labour is not in vain". When Neville had left, we all concluded that the Lord was underlining the rightness of the new step we were about to take.

Later, Neville called to ask me if I would lead the prayers of thanksgiving at Lily's funeral. Before he went, without knowing our plans and ideas, he gave us a prophetic word, "I think Lily will not be the last person you look after!"

The day before the telephone call from Bexhill Hospital, Bishop Peter came to supper. When we went into our sitting room for coffee, he picked up from the table a copy of the annual report of a hospice. He then introduced the subject of the need for a hospice in the area! With this unexpected turn of events, we shared our hospice thoughts. We described the vision we had been given for running a hospice in Bexhill, staffed by people living a corporate and apostolic life. Bishop Peter responded enthusiastically and suggested that, before proceeding any further, we should get in touch with Dr. Vaughan.

So we wrote to Dr. Vaughan and had a very quick response. He telephoned us to ask if he could come to visit in a week's time. He would like to bring a friend and ex-colleague with him, Dr. Keith Bradford.

We shared with them the vision that had grown from our experience of nursing Lily. We explained how we realised there was much more involved in looking after the terminally ill than physical nursing. Medically, Lily had needed the reassurance and advice of her own doctor, whom she knew well. His visits gave her confidence. Spiritually, she benefited greatly from her own minister being able to visit her freely. Emotionally, she enjoyed visits from friends who could come and go as they chose. She had needed the security of living in a place where she felt at home and could join in with our Jerusalem family life when she was well enough to do so.

The hospice we had in mind would seek to meet all these needs. Patients would be looked after by their own doctors. Their ministers would be free to visit at any time – friends and relatives too. One of our aims would be to relieve close relatives of the burden of heavy nursing so that it was possible for them to have a good night's sleep. We hoped that refreshed and strengthened, they could visit for long periods during the day. We would welcome them to take part in normal, homely activities with those they loved.

We wanted to help patients to lead as good a quality of life as possible. We also wanted to provide the security of a loving atmosphere in which they could face the future with confidence.

Dr. Vaughan and Dr. Bradford identified with our vision. They seemed excited by our ideas and offered their advice and support. They emphasised that we should start in a small way, suggesting that in the early stages we made provision for two or three patients.

The following Sunday on my way to a service at Beulah, I noticed a 'for sale' notice outside the house on the corner opposite to the church. At the time I was part of a Beulah committee discussing the provision of a home for elderly church members. It passed through my mind that this house would be ideal. Close to the church, frail people would be able to make their own way to services and church activities. I thought I might float this idea with other committee members.

Before I could do this, to my surprise Neville Barnett telephoned early the next morning to say a suitable property had been found. The exploratory committee would now be disbanded. Future affairs would be managed by a small business committee. This was an extraordinary moment of truth. I saw the house could be for the hospice instead and that I had been relieved of one responsibility to put my energies into another.

The same afternoon Sister Eva and I viewed the house. It had spacious light rooms. As far as we could tell it would be quite easy to convert into a hospice.

We recounted the happenings of the previous few weeks to all the Servants with Jesus. They were unanimous in believing the Lord was calling us to take a new step of faith and that He had been preparing us to do this. As we prayed together, we were given a scripture promise for the future, "My people will abide in a peaceful habitation, in secure dwellings and in quiet resting places" Isaiah 32:18. I could see that in looking after the dying we would be ministering to the Lord Himself.

The next day Dr. Vaughan and Dr. Bradford came to see over the house. We needed their professional opinion as to its suitability. They considered the house had very real possibilities and thought it would be worthwhile to have the property surveyed. Dr. Vaughan gave us a word of blessing before he left, "May God grant you your heart's desire and fulfil all your plans" Psalm 20:4.

Peter Evenden came within a few days to do a survey. He reported that the building was in good condition for its' age. There were no serious structural problems. When we shared this news with John Bickersteth he was very keen for us to go ahead.

Before making an offer for the house, we thought we should ask the Lord for a seal of £5,500 in our building society account. We were short of this by £1,300. Within a week we had received two cheques for £500 each and one for £300!

By the beginning of March, the trustees decided we should offer £45,000 for the house. The vendor said we could have the house for £46,000 including curtains and carpets; also on condition that the sale was a cash purchase and that we agreed to lose the deposit should the sale not go through. We accepted these conditions.

On 14th May, Rother District Council's Planning Committee gave permission for the house to be used as a hospice. When Peter Evenden received the official planning consent, he said he would be ready within a week to send out tender documents to builders, for the alterations that would be needed to convert the building. Events moved rapidly. The same day, we received the contract for the house from our solicitor for the trustees to sign. Twelve days later, the solicitor telephoned to say that contracts had been exchanged and completion day had been fixed for 25th June.

At the beginning of the month we had still needed £34,000 to complete the purchase. Specific prayer had been made for the release of money and workers. A few days before completion was due, the necessary funds were available. We received numerous donations ranging from £5,000 to £1. Some of these were anonymous. The balance was met by an interest-free loan.

By 22nd June, we were in a position to write a cheque for our solicitor. Sister Eva and I went to the early Communion service at St. Peter's, to offer the cheque, our letter to the solicitor and the future, to the Lord. We knelt at the Communion rail between two of Bishop Peter's Schemers, Simon and Geoff. They were at St. Peter's to bring joy to the parish and were later to become involved with our life at the hospice. As we knelt, the sun shone brightly across our letter. It seemed to us that God was promising His blessing on the future.

All went well on completion day. By midday we were in possession of the keys. At the end of the afternoon some of the Servants and Seventies went to occupy the house. Our arrival was well advertised. Sister Dorothy Mary Osborn and her husband, John, were with us. John was always interested in how things worked. When he turned on a switch he set off the fire alarm! We were unable to stop it ringing and had to send for an electrician. The alarm rang for about an hour. Neighbours came out into the road and people living in the flats opposite onto their balconies. All the neighbourhood knew we had arrived!

When all the excitement had died down, Michael Townroe called to see how we were getting on. Before leaving we had a time of prayer and thanksgiving in the kitchen.

Four days later we met with our trustees and Peter Evenden on site to discuss the alterations to the house. Downstairs the kitchen needed enlarging by knocking down the larder and walk-in cupboard walls. We wanted to add a sun lounge to the large downstairs sitting room for the benefit of patients who were well enough to get up for part of the day. Upstairs we planned to have two double rooms for patients and one single room. Fire regulations required us to build an adequate fire escape leading from one of the double bedrooms. We also needed to convert one small room into a sluice and another into an office for nurses on duty. Several builders had returned tender documents. We were unanimous in deciding to engage Stones of Hastings.

I made two interesting discoveries in the house. One was a small Jerusalem cross hidden away in a drawer. The other was a motto which had belonged to the small prep school that had previously used the house, "Via, Veritas, Vita", meaning "the Way, the Truth and the Life". It was good to know that Christians had previously occupied the house. We decided to call the hospice, the "Jerusalem Hospice".

Denis Ball stayed with us at Jerusalem several times during 1981. He always came with helpful words of encouragement and exhortation. On one of these occasions, he led several days of prayer and ministry for the Servants and Seventies. We talked about the future of Jerusalem and the Jerusalem Hospice. Denis emphasised the importance of looking out for people who longed to be wholly committed to the Lord and His vision.

Those whom God was calling were disclosed to us one by one. Dorothy Baker, one of the Seventies, who had given us mammoth support in looking after Lily, was one of the first. During May, she came to the conclusion that she should be selling her house and living at the Coach House. She could then be more involved with looking after the nurses and auxiliaries who would be living at Jerusalem. It would also free her to sometimes help at the hospice. She shared with Sister Eva and me that she believed she should put her house on the market the day the hospice was purchased. She wanted the proceeds from the sale of her house to go towards the cost of alterations. This was certainly total commitment!

Dorothy was a wonderful gift from God. Throughout the summer, she helped us with many of the practical preparations for the hospice as well as continuing to take a major role in the ever-growing amount of hospitality provided at the Coach House. It became increasingly obvious to us and to Dorothy that the Lord was calling her to be a Servant with Jesus. Her anointing and commissioning took place at Jerusalem in the prayer room during a Communion service attended by Servants and Seventies. From that time, Dorothy was known as Sister Dorothy Ellen to distinguish her from the other two Dorothys who were Servants

Ian McCulloch, with his wife Sister Phyllis, were staying with us for several days. He presided at the service and anointed Sister Dorothy Ellen for the ministry of helps. Ian spoke from Mark 8:34, "If any man would come after Me, let him deny himself and take up his cross and follow Me". An offering was made at the service in thanksgiving for all God was doing. It totalled £614 – exactly what we needed to pay for the hospice builders' first account, due the following day.

While we were looking after Lily we came to know Dr. Michael Robinson. He was very interested in the growing movement to care for the terminally ill in a hospice environment He knew our ideal plan was to have patients looked after by their own doctors. He realised this might not be possible for all general practitioners so he offered to take medical responsibility for their patients. Michael Robinson's offer was the beginning of a fruitful working relationship, particularly for Sister Eva and the nurses.

During the summer, Sister Eva and I had two special opportunities to learn more about hospice work. One was a day's visit to St. Christopher's Hospice. This was an excellent day for us, organised by Mary Baines, a consultant, whom I had known well from my university days in the

Christian Union. She arranged for us to meet staff involved in various aspects of the work. We were also invited to sit in on staff discussions about the best way to meet the immediate needs of individual patients.

Our second opportunity was through contact with Dr. Alan Kingsbury, director of the work at St. Barnabas' Hospice on the outskirts of Worthing. We were put in touch with him through Peter Evenden, whose son-in-law was a co-elder with him of the Baptist church at Durrington. He invited Sister Eva and me to lunch and to see over the hospice and to meet some of his staff. As a result the matron invited Sister Eva to stay with them for several days, to join her in her office work and home visits to prospective patients. Sister Eva took advantage of this generous suggestion. She gained much from this experience and was asked if she would like our nurses to make similar visits.

The first nurse who was willing to commit herself totally to our life and work was Hazel Morgan. She visited us a number of times, both at the Coach House and the hospice. In August, she telephoned to say she would like to take up the offer of a visit to St. Barnabas. She was seriously thinking of being available by November for work at the Jerusalem Hospice. In October, she went to St. Barnabas and in due course, committed herself to give a year to sharing our life at the Coach House and working in the hospice. Hazel proved a great strength to the team and stayed with us for the best part of two years.

Throughout the summer and autumn, the Lord sent a varied work force to help us with the very hard task of getting the hospice ready.

Some of the helpers were Seventies, working overtime. They took on new assignments in addition to their Coach House duties. Douglas Noble assisted with unpacking and fixing equipment as it arrived. He helped with such items as bedside lockers, electric bells for the patients, wall lights and five new hospital beds – the latest Nesbit Evans' model. John Osborn worked very hard in the garden, cutting back overgrown bushes and trees, clearing Yorkstone paths of moss and transforming grass which looked like a meadow, into a lawn.

Eileen Cox and Audrey Meyers did valiant work in the front garden. They were two state enrolled nurses who were interested in doing part time work in the hospice when it was opened. They pruned rose bushes and disentangled plants and bulbs in a well stocked garden. The plants were gradually being suffocated by weeds.

In the autumn we had reinforcements from the Schemers. Simon and Geoff were already supporting us. Then the second group of girls – Jane, Mary and Gerry – arrived at the beginning of September to live with us for ten weeks in Jerusalem. We followed the same pattern of worship and corporate life as before. They were good cooks and produced some excellent meals. Sister Eva taught them to make bread and they kept us well supplied. Their contribution to hospice preparations was considerable. They helped Sister Dorothy Ellen alter and make curtains for the spacious windows. They resurrected a large gas oven which we inherited from the previous school owners. One of the builders helped them dismantle the different parts for cleaning as it was covered with grease and grime. When their work was finished, the oven was gleaming, almost as new.

Jane, Mary and Gerry were lively and full of fun. They gave balance to our lives at a time when we could easily have become overwhelmed by our hospice commitments. They brought happiness to us, our helpers and our visitors. We also enjoyed getting to know the second group of young men on the Scheme. Under the direction of Vickery House, the incumbent of Berwick, all the Schemers went to Taize for a week. One evening early in November the young men arrived at the Coach House for supper. They had an early night, camping downstairs so that they could set out in good time to catch the boat to France. They all had breakfast in the middle of the night and started on their journey at about three o'clock in the morning. They returned a week later tired but radiant.

The second group of Bishop Peter's Schemers

Mary baking bread.

Gerry and Jane relaxing.

For the next few days, the girls sang Taize chants and songs around Jerusalem as they worked. In the middle of November, they left us to bring joy to the parish of St. Leonards, Seaford and Sister Dorothy Ellen moved into Jerusalem to be settled in and ready for the blessing of the hospice.

Before the blessing, we received a generous donation of £12,210. This marvellous gift more than covered the cost of all the new hospice equipment.

St. Andrew's day arrived and Bishop Peter came to bless the newly furnished and renovated hospice. As he prayed in all the rooms, he commented on how beautiful everything looked. At the front door he named the house the "Jerusalem Hospice".

A wonderful gathering of the Lord's people was drawn together that day. The Servants and Seventies were there with our trustees and pastoral advisers. All those who helped with the preparations of the hospice came, including some of the Schemers. For those who had offered to serve in the hospice, this was a special day of commitment.

The afternoon finished with a time of praise and prayer in the main sitting room and a short address by Bishop Peter. He spoke about loving and caring and how we would only be able to do this fully, through the resurrection life given to us in Christ, through His dying. We truly care by meeting people where they are.

Bishop Peter concluded by saying, "In the hospice you will be living in no-man's-land, between earth and heaven. No-man's-land is a dangerous and exciting place to be!"

Chapter Nineteen

Living in No-Man's-Land

"you have come .... to the city of the living God, the heavenly Jerusalem."
Hebrews 12:22

For two and a half years, we found ourselves living in a kind of no man's land, in two dimensions, one very earthed; the other bringing us close to heaven.

In our earthly Jerusalem at the Coach House, we entered into a new phase of corporate community life. At the Jerusalem hospice, although there was much basic unpleasant work to be done, the company of heaven never seemed far away.

After the hospice blessing, we decided to have a pause for two months before receiving patients. It seemed important to strengthen our relationships with members of the public. We wanted to give an opportunity for people to look over the house and see the facilities on offer. We also needed to enlarge our team of part-time volunteers, to ensure that the full-time staff had plenty of support. This plan produced some excellent results.

One volunteer who offered part-time nursing assistance was Sheila Leach. She was keen to gather a group of people together to start a hospice in Hastings. She asked if she could join us to gain as much experience as possible We became a mutual help and encouragement to each other. In due course she became the prime mover in establishing St. Michael's Hospice.

We were ready to receive patients by the beginning of February. Sister Eva took the position of sister-in-charge. When we started planning for the hospice, she had not envisaged herself in this role. Neither of us had seen ourselves being so fully involved on a daily basis. It became clear, however, that the Servants with Jesus themselves should take overall responsibility for different aspects of work, if the vision was to be fulfilled.

Sister Eva's role was to lead the nursing team and liaise closely with doctors and relatives. My role was to be in charge of housekeeping at the hospice and to organise the back-up team for the nurses. They needed at least one person on the premises twenty-four hours a day. During the daytime, the nurses needed the help of several volunteers.

Sister Dorothy Ellen's role was to be in charge of housekeeping at the Coach House. She looked after our ever-increasing number of visitors and the full-time resident hospice team.

On 5th February 1982, our first patient arrived. Sister Eva had already visited him and his wife in their home. He was a very frightened gentleman in his mid-sixties. He asked Sister Eva to promise he would never be left alone and that no one would preach to him. She promised his requests would be respected. Simon, one of the Schemers, helped with the nursing. He also kept the patient's mind occupied by talking on many topics – including football!

Our patient lived for three and a half weeks. The staff developed a very good rapport with him and his wife. Halfway through his time with us, he had a bad night. It was my turn to be on support duty the following evening. Both the nurse and myself felt that we should ask him if he would like us to pray for a good night's sleep. He seemed pleased and agreed. We said a brief prayer, the Lord's prayer and a blessing. He slept well. From that time, we prayed with him every evening. We noticed that he began to say the Lord's prayer and the blessing with us. One evening he said to the nurse on duty, "God bless you, my dear!"

A few nights on, Sister Eva and Simon were sitting by the patient's bed. They both experienced a tremendous sense of the Lord's presence. The patient then asked, "Who is the man standing in the corner?" Sister Eva was moved to say, "It is the Lord Jesus Who has come to help you on the last part of your journey." From that moment he entered into a deep peace which did not leave him until he died three days later. This was one of a number of awe-inspiring experiences we had as we worked in no-man's-land.

Caring for our first patient was a valuable preparation for our future busy life. The whole experience helped us to understand more fully the needs of the dying and those facing bereavement. It also helped us in our planning of a suitable routine for the Jerusalem Hospice and for our corporate life at the Coach House.

The changeover from night to day duty took place at eight o'clock. Those going on duty committed the day to the Lord. Doctors often called on their way to morning surgery. Decisions would then be made about the best treatment for each patient for the coming day.

We aimed to have patients washed, dressed and comfortable in time to listen to the BBC's New Every Morning service. We found patients liked to listen to this programme. It gave them a starting point when they wanted to talk about matters of faith and did not know where to begin. There was so much interest that we bought copies of the New Every Morning book so that those who wished, could follow the service and read the prayers for themselves.

Night duty started at eight o'clock and was the responsibility of a nurse supported by an auxiliary. After settling the patients for the night, the auxiliaries slept when possible. The nurses would wake them for drug rounds and sometimes to be company for dying patients. Sister Dorothy Ellen, myself and Sister Edna with her husband, George, undertook the major part of this work. Some of our assignments were exacting but we found them very rewarding and a great privilege. It was during the nights that we grew close to the patients and experienced most the reality of being in no-man's-land.

Everyone who served at the hospice or at the Coach House did so without salary. They regarded what they were doing as part of their service to the Lord. We did not charge patients fees. As at the Coach House, we offered our service freely in the name of the Lord. We welcomed donations from those who wished to give. Those who could offer nothing or very little, had exactly the same treatment as those who were in a position to offer much. We were never without the financial resources we needed.

The majority of our part-time volunteers belonged to different churches in Bexhill. Others came from further afield – mostly from Hastings, St. Leonards and Eastbourne. The main input however was from the full-time nurses and auxiliaries who committed themselves to sharing life at our Coach House Jerusalem.

An extraordinary variety of people were sent to be "Jerusalem Dwellers", as they were later called. Some came for a few months; others for two years or so. Amongst the nurses was Catherine who had been working at Lee Abbey. Shelagh added spiritual strength to our household and was tireless in the contributions she made at the hospice. She worked with the Church Missionary Society and had been refused a visa to return to Gambia at the end of her furlough. She remained until the way was opened for her to return. Gaynor, recently returned from the Sudan, was delightfully relaxed and caring. She stayed with us for nearly two years. Janet served several months, until sadly her own health prevented her from continuing the heavy hospice work.

Auxiliaries came from different parts of the world to share our Jerusalem life. There was Katrine, a lovely young Swiss woman, who planned to be an occupational therapist. She brought much joy to the patients. She was very gifted musically. Her singing and guitar-playing helped to inspire our daily worship. Rayko, a Japanese doctor joined us for six months. It was the custom in Japan for doctors never to tell their patients that they were dying. When Rayko became a Christian, she wanted to learn how Christian doctors and nurses ministered to the dying; so she came to live and work with us. Mary came to us from the United States. She was a mature, caring, sensitive person who brought quality to our social and corporate life. She was often responsible for lively discussions at meal times. We also had three Malaysian Chinese sixth formers, who used to join us for several weeks at Christmas and Easter. They were from a Methodist girls' school in Kent. They were considering becoming doctors. One of them went on to study at Medical school in Dundee. They were sometimes homesick but they had a lovely sense of humour and enriched our community life. A highlight for us all was when one of them, from a Buddhist background, asked to be baptised as a believer.

With such a mixture of backgrounds and cultures, it was very important for us to have a commonly understood basis for our corporate life. We needed to be strong together in the Lord, if we were to minister effectively to patients and to those facing bereavement. Sister Eva and I drew up twelve brief precepts and put them into leaflet form under the heading, 'Call and Aims for Jerusalem Dwellers'. Being human, we have often fallen short of these aims and we also discovered that our spiritual enemy hated them. They still form the basis of our corporate life in the Servants with Jesus.

Our different work schedules made it difficult for all Jerusalem Dwellers to be free for worship and prayer at the same time. All who were available met at seven o'clock before breakfast and at six o'clock before the evening meal. Meeting at the Lord's table together at least once a week was considered a priority. When Canon Derek Tansill had settled in as the new Rector of St. Peter's, we invited him to come and celebrate Communion for us in the Jerusalem prayer room. He arranged to come at seven o'clock on Tuesday mornings. We organised rotas so that all the Jerusalem Dwellers could be present. Derek usually stayed for breakfast. In this way, we grew to know him well. He was a great support and encouragement and brought colour and zest into our lives. His sense of humour and fund of true stories lifted our spirits for the day ahead.

Our corporate prayer life strengthened us as we travelled with those at the hospice journeying through no-man's-land. There were wonderful and new experiences but the journeys were sometimes difficult and puzzling. It was not easy to understand why those who came to us very sick and expected to die within a few days, lived for two or three months while others expected to live for several weeks, died within days. It was not easy to explain why a mother with young children died while one of our patients over eighty, expected to live at the very most for two weeks, left us a year later, totally healed.

Such happenings underlined for us that our times are truly in God's hands, that His priorities and purposes are different from ours. On reflection, we could sometimes see possible answers to our queries. Seen in the perspective of God's ultimate desire for everyone to know Him and to be reconciled to Him and one another, some events could be understood. It seemed that when and how patients died or lived, was ordered in such a way that each had the maximum opportunity to know God for themselves.

One very sick patient was so ill that we did not expect her to live for more than twenty-four hours. Bishop Peter visited us that day. He celebrated Communion in her room and he anointed her, offering prayers for her strengthening as she journeyed to God. We expected her to die during the night. I was amazed when I went on duty the next morning to find her eating breakfast. It was important that she lived for a few more weeks. During that time, her son and two daughters who had not spoken to each other for years, were reconciled as their visits to their mother coincided.

Seen with the human eye alone, it was a tragedy when the mother of two young children died. There was however a very special opportunity a few days before her death, for the whole family to come into the Lord's presence and be given Christian hope and comfort. The patient's sister and brother-in-law visited on Easter Sunday afternoon. Her sister asked in the early evening whether it would be possible, as it was Easter day, to have Communion. I knew that the evening service at Beulah -just across the road – would soon be finishing with Communion. At the end of the service, Neville Barnett would come to the church door before the rest of the congregation. If I waited in the porch, it would be possible to have a quick word with him. I waited and was able to explain the situation to him. He quickly grasped the need. When Beulah members had dispersed, he came across to the hospice.

In the meanwhile, Sister Eva had prepared the patient, the family and the room ready for a short service. As well as the patient's sister and brother-in-law, other family members were present – her young husband and her two teenage sons from a previous marriage, wearing earrings and dressed in leather jackets. Neville gave them hope and comfort for the future. When he came into the room he said, "This evening we celebrate the first Easter Sunday evening, when Jesus appeared after His resurrection in the Upper Room to His disciples. His first words to them were, 'Peace be with you!' He says the same words to us this evening in this upper room. He does not want us to be afraid." A few days later, the patient died peacefully.

Why was a patient over eighty healed? Only God Himself fully knows the answer. Possibly, it was because she moved from complete unbelief to know the Lord personally for herself. It was important for others that she lived to share her testimony.

When this patient came into the hospice she had given up her home and disposed of her possessions. She was expected to die within a few days from lung cancer. She made it very clear that she did not want 'any religion' as she put it. A few weeks later, she was strong enough to get out of bed without help. We noticed that just before the morning service, she was giving out the service books to the other patients. Four months on, Sister Eva was moved to give her a cross from the Palm Sunday service. Our patient used it as a book marker! After Easter, she drew Sister Eva aside and said, "I want you to know, Sister, that this is the best Easter I have ever had – and I am not just saying it to please you!" By the autumn, X-rays proved that her lungs were completely free from cancer. We found her a suitable place to move to in a small rest home in the centre of Bexhill. She was able to go out and about and do her own shopping.

Some months later, I was asked to speak at a Senior Citizens' meeting in Bexhill. In a question time, a rather cynical gentleman said, "Do you preach at patients in the hospice?" "No!" I said and told the story of the patient who was healed. Someone in the audience said, "We know all about that! She came back to the warden-care flats where she lived to tell us all about her new faith and how God had healed her!"

I could share with you about other journeys through no-man's-land – each one special and unique. It was apparent that many of those who journeyed met with the Lord at their point of need. Most of the travellers ended their earthly journeys in peace as God spoke to them and made Himself known.

We were able to nurse approximately fifty patients during the life of the hospice. There was much happiness in this ministry. So often visitors commented on the atmosphere of peace and joy. It was a great sadness when we realised that we might not be able to maintain the ministry indefinitely.

The main cause for this was the gradual dispersal of most of the Jerusalem Dwellers and nurses. For some, God opened up new callings and opportunities. In 1985 Sister Dorothy Ellen, to everyone's joy and delight married Frank Sharp. Kay Mullins, one of our key part-time nurses who used to deputise as sister-in-charge for Sister Eva, moved to Midhurst. Shelagh Jebb obtained her long-awaited visa to return to Gambia. Gaynor Christensen felt she should train as a midwife with a view to serving abroad. Hazel Morgan had long overstayed her original offer to help for a year.

We knew that unless these committed state registered nurses were replaced, we could not carry on. In 1986, Rosemary Duncan joined us with a view to becoming sister-in-charge. After several months of waiting and prayer, no suitably qualified nurses came forward to assist her. We all concluded that the time to close the Jerusalem Hospice had come.

God's guidance in this matter was very clear. He could so easily have called a new wave of Jerusalem Dwellers. If we had paid salaries, we might well have been able to attract nurses but to run a commercial enterprise was not what we felt called to do.

When Bishop Peter came to bless the Jerusalem Hospice, St. Michael's Hospice at St. Leonards and St. Wilfrid's at Eastbourne did not exist. We felt that in some small measure, we had pioneered hospice work in the area and now was the time to relinquish the work to others.

We were pleased that we were able to sell the hospice to a Christian nurse who wanted to start a small, homely nursing home. With the proceeds, we gave donations to St. Michael's and St. Wilfrid's. We also gave a donation to St. Barnabas' in appreciation of all the help they gave to our nurses. We were able to repay the balance we owed on our interest-free loan. One of our generous donors said he would like the contribution he had made to be used for the wider work of the Servants with Jesus.

With the closing of the Jerusalem Hospice, Sister Eva and I were set free for new areas of service. For both of us, the hospice years gave invaluable experience for our future ministries. Sister Eva became a member of the Hospital Chaplaincy team. Some of my future parish work would be with the sick, the dying and the bereaved.

Chapter Twenty

New Beginnings

" ....fulfil your ministry" 2 Timothy 4:5

"You will minister with My priests, in My sanctuary, to the glory of My name".

These words came strongly into my mind totally unrelated to any previous thoughts. I was kneeling at the communion rail in St. Peter's at a Sunday parish Communion service on St. Stephen's day 1982. The Spirit seemed to be bringing to my notice that everyone else kneeling at the rail was a choir member. They and everyone in the sanctuary were wearing some kind of distinctive clothing. It was then that the unexpected words formed in my mind. They were accompanied by a sensation of being drawn into the ministering body.

I can remember being filled with joy, feeling that the Lord was going to do something special amongst us at St. Peter's. The idea of ordination did not enter my head. I began to think about the healing ministry. I envisaged myself and other laity helping with the laying-on-of-hands and prayer for the sick. I wrote the words I had been given in my diary but did not share them with anyone.

When Derek Tansill arrived in the parish he quickly began to mobilise the members of St. Peter's. At his first annual general meeting, he told us that his top priority was going to be to help everyone to reach their fullest potential. He intended to use the laity as much as possible. He started to do as he had promised. For me personally, within a few months, I was leading intercessions, I was responsible for a house group and tutoring a group for the Bishop's Certificate course.

During August I went to stay at Crowhurst Home of Healing for a week. I needed a pause. I was very exhausted by the continuing hospice ministry and corporate life at the Coach House. Many marvellous things had happened since my commissioning to go out into East Sussex. There had however been a number of hurts and disappointments. I was sometimes confronted with an incredible lack of love and unity amongst God's people which I found distressing. The new openings at St. Peter's were exhilarating.

They seemed to fulfil John Bickersteth's challenge of years ago, to engage in a ministry of prayer and the word. I needed time to draw aside to think and pray.

As I was shown into my room at Crowhurst, I felt enveloped in the , embrace and love of God. The Spirit seemed to be touching and healing the roots of pain inside and I wept with joy and relief. For a few minutes, I had a sharpened awareness. Everything around me looked so beautiful. The breeze stirring the trees outside, gave the impression of moving with the stirring of the Holy Spirit.

Throughout my stay, I took part in the corporate worship in the main chapel. Otherwise I spent most of the mornings and evenings in my room. As the weather was fine and sunny, I spent the afternoons visiting and praying in the village churches in the Battle and Bexhill Deanery. Towards the end of the week, various strands were coming together in my mind. There was an increasing conviction that in any future ministry, there would be a strong element of reconciliation.

I talked over the things I had been shown with the Reverend David Payne who was, at the time, warden of the Home of Healing. As a result, he anointed me for a ministry of reconciliation. As David was praying, he was given several scriptures which filled me with expectancy and hope for the future:-

> "You will know the truth and the truth will make you free". John 8:32
> "I know the plans I have for you .... plans for welfare .... to give you a future and a hope." Jeremiah 29:11
> "Behold, I am doing a new thing; now it springs forth ...." Isaiah 43:19
> "Take heart, it is I; have no fear." Mark 6:50

Within a few days of returning to Jerusalem, a new pathway began to open. One morning after sharing in the Communion service and breakfast for Jerusalem Dwellers, Derek drew me aside. He asked me if I would consider being a minister of the Cup for the parish communion services.

Would you please think and pray about this?" he said. "I don't need to," I replied. "I already know the answer." I had had no thoughts or aspirations in this direction but what Derek was asking me to consider exactly described the insights given the previous St. Stephen's day. This invitation following so closely on my visit to Crowhurst, showed me that I was about to enter a completely new phase – whatever the hardships that lay ahead there would also be much joy and blessing.

I was commissioned for this new ministry with two others at a parish Communion service in November. I did not realise at the time but this was the beginning of the path that was eventually to lead to ordination.

In due course, Derek suggested that I should think seriously about being a lay reader. He said it was not good stewardship for my training and gifts of communication to be lost. The churchwardens supported Derek's proposition and Bishop Peter was enthusiastic about me going ahead. It was agreed that I should train with a view to being commissioned in the autumn of 1984. Derek arranged for me to have two tutors from very different traditions. I wrote essays on theological and pastoral topics and went fortnightly to discuss these with Father Derek Allen of St. Saviour's, Eastbourne. I prepared sermons to read to Canon Frank Colquhoun for comment. I felt privileged to have these two truly holy men of God helping me. They were encouraging and stimulating. As I listened and talked with them, I learned many new things.

In the middle of October, Bishop Peter admitted me to be a reader as 'Sister Eileen'. This seemed exactly right as I would be serving in St. Peter's parish not only as a reader but also as a Servant with Jesus.

Becoming a reader was for me a tremendous milestone. All through the year of training, I had qualms that I might not make the grade. Imagine my consternation when a few days after my admission, Derek said this was just a be ginning. I chose not to comment and pushed his remark to the back of my mind.

I preached my first sermons at St. Peter's, the church of the Good Shepherd and St. Michael's during November. The months that followed were full, busy and satisfying. I took Communion to the sick in nursing homes and to people in their own homes. I organised the Pastoral Link visiting scheme for the whole parish. I was content in fulfilling all these duties. I felt I had now arrived and that I was where God wanted me to be. I envisaged continuing with complementary duties at the Coach House and in the parish indefinitely.

In April 1985, I was jolted out of this comfortable position. Eva Hammond-Lucy who had prayed regularly for me ever since I left the Grammar School, came to stay at Jerusalem for a few days' rest and refreshment. She was a reader, a converted Jewess and spoke with authority. She was the kind of person whose remarks one did not ignore. During her visit she suddenly said, "Eileen, I have been praying for you. For sometime now I keep on getting the impression that God is going to call you into ministry in the Anglican church. I am not exactly sure to what ministry but something like a Deaconess."

For two or three days, I could not get her remarks our of my mind. I had to weigh them carefully. On St. Mark's day, I went to the Communion service at St. Peter's to ask for specific guidance. I needed to know whether to pursue Eva's thoughts further. The epistle was from 2 Timothy, Chapter 4. As it was read, the words "fulfil your ministry" seemed to leap out of the page. My thoughts went right back to my initial call at the age of sixteen, to teach and preach the word of God. I could see that many things that had happened since had been preparing me for the ordained ministry within the church.

When I went to receive Communion, I found myself kneeling in the same place where God had spoken to me about serving in His sanctuary. As I realised this, two short sentences came into my mind, "This is where I called you. Go in peace!" I saw that two and half years earlier the Lord was speaking to me about the ordained ministry and I had failed to recognise it.

Metaphorically, I had cold feet and wanted to run away. I decided I must not do this but commit myself to going along this new and unexpected path if it was truly God's will. I went into the vestry after the service to share with Derek, Eva Hammond-Lucy's directives and the things I had just been shown. Derek's response was, "That is what I have been praying for!" We arranged to meet on the following Monday.

In the meantime, early on Sunday morning, I switched on the radio. Bishop Cormac Murphy-O'Connor, Roman Catholic Bishop of Arundel and Brighton, was talking about the priestly ministry and how Maundy Thursday unfolded for him so marvellously the meaning of that ministry. His words spoke to my heart and spirit. I had an inner knowing that the Lord was in fact calling me to the priestly ministry. I went to the prayer room and opened the Bible to read Isaiah Chapter 61. I had a sense of awe as I read words in verse 6 I had forgotten were there, "You shall be called the priests of the Lord, men shall speak of you as the ministers of our God." I shared these thoughts with Derek the next day and how I believed the Lord was calling me to be a priest. Derek very sensibly responded, "That is not possible at the moment! We must get on with what is possible!"

Events moved very rapidly in spite of discouraging information from Sister Marion Mingins, who was in charge of womens' ministry throughout the country. When I met her at Sussex University at the beginning of May, she told me that for the following autumn all places for training at theological colleges were already taken. Also there were no vacancies at selection conferences for ministry in the Church of England until October.

The Lord had other plans. Bishop Peter suggested that I went to Chichester Theological College. As I had a degree in theology and a wide teaching experience, I did not need to complete all the usual lecture courses. With my Free Church background, he thought my knowledge of liturgy was probably rather shaky; also I needed the opportunity to consider current ethical issues and pastoral needs. So Bishop Peter proposed that I should go to Chichester for a year and concentrate on these three areas of concern.

I went for interviews and was offered a place living out for the autumn term but living in college for the following two terms. This offer was with the proviso that I was recommended by the selection committee. Someone dropped out of the selection procedure. Thus wonderfully, I was able to attend a selection conference in September and take up my place at Chichester.

For the first term my main base was still in Jerusalem at Bexhill. I travelled to and fro twice a week. In January 1986, I took up residence in college. The first week was most unusual as all the students were occupied with examinations. They had no time for socialising. There were no lectures to attend. The second day I said to the Lord, "Why am I here? I could have been occupied more profitably back in Bexhill!"

Immediately there came into my mind the words of Bishop Peter when Sister Eva and I spoke to him about the blessing and naming of the Coach House. "Jerusalem it shall be! I think the name has a prophetic content." A train of thought continued, "We have been living the Jerusalem life now for more than seven years. We have learnt much. We had been shown something of God's intentions and loving purposes for His people – His Church – His New Jerusalem. We should share these. Should we give His people the opportunity to spend days at the Coach House thinking about their inheritance as members of the New Jerusalem? Should we be running a series of 'Jerusalem Seminars'?"

A whole series of human needs then presented themselves which I thought could be met by a deeper understanding of the Jerusalem life:

> The need to have a meaningful experience of community, companionship, solidarity, well-being and sharing so that death itself is a home coming; The need to be free from a sense of alienation, isolation and of feeling cut off from human and Divine contact and affection;
>
> The need for fears, doubts and ignorance to be removed; fear of death in particular, robs us of the richness of our Christian life now. We need to know the answer to the question, "What happens to me when I die?"
>
> The need to live in the reality of forgiveness, to be set free from bondages and to enter into healing relationships with those on earth and in heaven.

I concluded I should spend the examination week planning a series of seminars. At the end of the week, I shared my thoughts with John Hind, the college principal. I asked if instead of writing essays, I might develop the seminar themes. He gave his blessing to this idea and arranged for some of the staff to help me in tutorials.

Corporate life in the college was undergirded by a daily celebration of the Eucharist and by the Daily Offices. This was a pattern that was going to prove very strengthening in the days ahead and certainly increased my appreciation of liturgy.

All students were required to have a spiritual director. This was a new experience for me. As Father Derek Allen visited the college several times a term, I asked him if he would be able to undertake this responsibility. I was greatly relieved when his answer was, "Yes!" I owe much to his wisdom, kindness and understanding.

At the end of the summer term, Archbishop Michael Ramsay came to lead three days' retreat for leavers. Those were wonderful days. He was elderly and frail. He spoke to us from his throne-like seat. As we listened, I felt we must be experiencing something like the early Christians who sat at the feet of St. John the Apostle. The theme of his talks was truly marvellous and met my particular needs. Throughout my training, I had been a little anxious about the dual role I was to have as a Deacon and Servant with Jesus. Would I have time to do both? Would there be a clash of interests? Michael Ramsay began his talks with these words, "To be a Deacon is to be a Servant with Jesus!" His words dispersed all my anxieties. We spent the next three days thinking about what it meant to be a servant with Jesus.

Sadly, the legislation for women to become members of the Diaconate was much slower going through Parliament than anticipated. It was not possible for me to be ordained Deacon in July as originally planned. I had to wait for nearly eleven months before this was possible.

In spite of this disappointment, 3rd July 1986 was a great day. In the context of a Eucharist, I was admitted to the order of Deaconess by Bishop Peter at St. Peter's. The church was full of supportive Christian friends. It was one of those special occasions when we experienced much joy. As we sang the words of a Communion hymn, I felt I was embarking on a new and joyous journey:

> "Deck thyself, my soul, with gladness,
> Leave the gloomy haunts of sadness,
> Come into the daylight's splendour,
> There with joy thy praises render."

Chapter Twentyone

Released to be a Deacon

"If you continue in My word .... you will know the truth and the truth will make you free." John 8:31-32

The days that immediately followed the service of commissioning were days of fulfilment and joy. However, within a few weeks, there was considerable tension and conflict in my own personal circumstances.

I had, in measure, been prepared for this dual development, by prophetic words sent to me in a letter by Denis Ball on the day I was made a deaconess: "Go forward in My Name. Be strong in My strength, so that you may do battle with the enemy and not be afraid. See, I clothe you with a mantle which can never tarnish nor grow old, for I am life eternal. Daily walk with Me and let My shadow protect you from heat of selfishness and earthly desire. Drink from the cup of My suffering that your thirst may be quenched. Eat of My brokenness that your hunger may be satisfied. Taste and see that I am your manna in the wilderness .... as you have now been blessed so bless; in this manner you will know heavenly enrichment and joy." There were many positive openings. Our new Rector, John Cotton, who had replaced Derek during my absence at Chichester, gave plenty of opportunities for ministry. He gave me a full diaconal role at the parish Eucharist. I served throughout the service, reading the Gospel and giving the Dismissal. This was a tremendous privilege and gathered me up into a new closeness to the Lord and His people. I occasionally gave the ministry of the word and from time to time preached at Evensong.

The staff were expected to attend the daily Communion service and daily Evensong. We were each responsible for leading Evensong on a weekly basis. This discipline was strengthening and undergirded everything we did. Praying together twice a day kept us in touch with one another and provided the opportunity for exchange of news and to ask advice.

Early in the autumn, John asked me if I would take on the responsibility of resourcing the parish house groups and look for openings to initiate new ones. He also extended my ministry of taking Communion to rest and nursing homes and to housebound parishioners.

While I was still at Chichester, John started a monthly Communion service with prayer for healing. He had collected together a team of a dozen or so parishioners to assist with the laying-on-of-hands. This excited me as it was exactly what I had seen with my mind's eye four years previously on St. Stephen's day. The team met a few days before each service to prepare. It was not long before the preparation meetings took place at the Coach House. We met at eight o'clock on a Saturday in the prayer room for Communion, followed by breakfast and discussion. Decisions were made about the theme of the service and the different tasks we would undertake.

The early months after my return from Chichester were very positive, largely due to all the openings John gave. I count myself fortunate to have had this encouragement. Some of my women contemporaries did not experience such wide open doors for service.

There were however some very negative pressures in my personal circumstances. I was in the middle of a family crisis. My mother had been in hospital for five months with a badly broken leg after a severe fall. My father's situation seemed desperate and he was keen for me to return home to look after them. This presented a conflict of loyalties. Then there were people in my immediate scene in Bexhill who were aggressive towards women in public ministry. There were also others who coveted the Coach House for their own use, to fulfil their own ambitions. All these things were emotionally undermining and draining.

I was so concerned that I telephoned Denis. I wanted to ask for his insights in the light of the prophetic words he had sent. He helped me to see what was happening in the perspective of spiritual warfare. He said that I needed to recognise the tactics of the evil one and then mobilise the forces in Christ against him. About those creating the difficulties, he said, "Do not concentrate on asking for specific things for individuals but bless them in the Name of the Lord. He wants to give them much more than we do! Bless! However much the individual does not want the blessings, blessings are always creative, cursings destructive."

Denis emphasised the importance of daily walking close to the Lord. In this way His shadows would protect me and the selfishness, earthly desires, jealousies and ambitions of others would not be able to touch me. He spoke of being totally allied to the will of God, seeking to bear Christ's yoke with Him, allowing His way to operate and to accept what He permits. "In harness with Him the yoke is easy and the burden light."

These words were a light on my path, not just for the immediate future but for the whole future. It was absolutely clear that I should pursue the path towards being a deacon and trust God to sort things out for those around me.

Bishop Eric of Chichester arranged for the first women deacons in the diocese to be ordained on 14th May 1987, the feast of St. Matthias. This assumed an extraordinary significance. It was as though in some sense we were destined, like St. Matthias, to fill gaps in the ministry of the church. Arrangements were made for us to be ordained in three different groups within the three archdeaconries in which we were to serve.

These services were preceded by three special days of retreat at the convent of the Community of the Holy Family at St. Mary's, Baldslow. The weather was perfect. The large overgrown grounds were very, very beautiful. We experienced May at its very best. There were carpets of bluebells at every turn and the old apple trees in the orchard were covered with blossom. One afternoon while walking through this lovely wilderness, with the birds singing, I came unexpectedly upon the graveyard for the sisters. A deep tranquillity descended. It was as though heaven and earth were meeting. The past and present were somehow brought together in that moment. Christian women who had served the Lord faithfully in former days seemed joined in spirit with those who were seeking to serve Him late in the twentieth century.

Sister Hazel of the Community of St. Margaret's, East Grinstead, led the retreat, she wonderfully affirmed our callings and gave us much encouragement. Two of her remarks have stayed with me. The first was about humility, "True humility is to take the authority given and use it." The second remark put the purpose of ordination into perspective, "Ordination and your life of prayer, are so that you may be an open pathway for God's Spirit to come to His people – then it won't matter what happens to you in the future! It is important that your people take knowledge of you that you have been with Jesus."

The ordination service for the East Sussex deacons took place at the parish church of St. Leonard, Seaford. This arrangement could not have been better from my point of view. It meant that my father was able to be present. Inspite of his frailty, he was still an elder of the United Reformed Church in Chelmsford. His minister, Rev. Geoffrey Roper, had previously been the United Reformed minister at Seaford and had worked closely with the vicar in ecumenical affairs. Geoffrey telephoned me a few days before the ordination. He asked if I would like him to bring my father and a friend, Aimee Bass, who had prayed for me since I was a teenager, to the service. This was a wonderful proposition. My father had gradually changed over the months and become enthusiastic about the prospect of my ordination. The vicar gave them a warm welcome and arranged for them to sit in the pew just behind me.

The ordination day was one of great happiness and fulfilment. It was marvellous to be surrounded by the love of many friends. At the ordination, the Holy Spirit imparted a cool, refreshing, healing peace, releasing me for future ministry. When I preached at Evensong the following Sunday, I knew an inner confidence and authority that I had not known before. Others may not have been conscious of the difference but the new awareness within has never left me.

The months that followed were filled with opportunities to draw alongside people. Taking baptisms, confirmation classes, funerals and an occasional wedding made it possible to share meaningfully at the point of people's needs and joys. I thoroughly enjoyed preparing people for baptism and confirmation.

My life in the parish was closely interwoven with life at the Coach House.

This made sense as Offa's gift of land included both the present Manor site and St. Peter's. Also the inspiration for the Servants with Jesus had been the day of prayer for women in May 1971. This had started in the Manor Barn and finished in St. Peter's church. Words of promise from the prophet Ezekiel had, for years, been important to the Servants as they prayed for all who lived, worked and worshipped on the hill in Bexhill Old Town. "I will make them and the places round My hill a blessing; and I will send down the showers in their season; they shall be showers of blessing." Ezekiel 34:26.

The fortnightly parish Bible studies took place in Jerusalem. John asked me to take responsibility for these. The Coach House was also a suitable, informal venue for confirmation classes. While a new community centre was being built for St. Peter's, some of the church activities that usually took place there, were held at the Coach House.

Personally, I was still engaged in activities that presented themselves and touched areas of East Sussex far beyond Bexhill. I became tutor to three men training to become non-stipendary priests – Geoffrey France came from Uckfield, Douglas Caffyn from Eastbourne and Frank Rowson from Hastings. For three years we met weekly at the Coach House. This was a learning process for all of us and I believe we learnt much from each other. Sadly we missed Frank from our last tutorials as his secular work took him for a time to Cambridgeshire. At the end of the course, all three men were ordained to serve in East Sussex. Geoffrey is now serving in the stipendary ministry as Rector of Warbleton and Bodle Street Green.

Soon after returning from Chichester, I began to use the material prepared for Jerusalem seminars. Participants came once a month for nine months to the Coach House from ten o'clock to three o'clock. The theme of the day was introduced, followed by two hours of private prayer and Bible study. After a picnic lunch, discoveries were shared together in the prayer room. The sessions ended with a time of prayer for one another.

The seminars have proved popular. We still run these courses as the need arises. The aim of Jerusalem seminars is twofold; first to help Christians to discover and enter into their full inheritance as citizens of the New Jerusalem; secondly to identify one another's God-given ministries. A number of Servants with Jesus have helped with the leading of the groups.

There were several highlights in 1988, both in the parish and at the Coach House. In the parish, we had a special day of renewal in June led by Denis Ball. This was in preparation for a parish weekend in September to be held at Pilgrim Hall. Denis spoke about the Holy Spirit filling us with His divine life and love. The day ended in the church where we each lit a candle to symbolise our desire to be lights in the world. This was a time of much blessing with a strong awareness of the Lord's presence.

John invited a close friend of his, the Rev. John Barter from Hounslow, to lead the parish weekend. He brought a small team from his own parish to support him. Seventy to eighty St. Peter's parishioners, both young and old, took part. It was a weekend of immense blessing, far beyond my greatest expectations. On Saturday evening, the Holy Spirit moved amongst us touching and transforming lives as on the first day of Pentecost. Some people were changed dramatically beyond the point of return.

The highlight of the year at the Coach House was the visit of overseas bishops around the time of the Lambeth Conference. We gave hospitality to Bishop Samuel and his wife from Nigeria. They stayed with us for ten days while they visited church fellowships in the Battle and Bexhill and Rye deaneries. They needed much tender loving care as it was their first visit to the United Kingdom. They had difficulty in coping with our climate and rich food. It was a challenge to be with a bishop whose diocese was so poor that he had borrowed a bishop's cassock which was much too big for him, to wear at the conference. Sister Eva undertook the mammoth task of alteration before he left us. Samuel was a man of much faith and an inspiration to all. Two of his main concerns were how to provide enough food to prevent his people from starving and how to provide his pastors and evangelists with sufficient transport in a very rural area. How different from the concerns of our own bishops! Subsequently the two deaneries who entertained Samuel and his wife were able to provide his diocese with a new car.

We also had the joy of entertaining three bishops from Burma for the day. They made the journey from London, specially to visit Anne Emmens, one of the Seventies, who later became Sister Anna of the Servants with Jesus. She had spent most of her working life in Burma as a missionary. Bishop Timothy of Mandalay had been in her Bible class as a boy of fourteen. He and his friends, Bishop Andrew and Bishop Barnabas came to say, "Thank you!" for all Anne had done for their people.

Two weeks after Easter 1989, I went to stay with Derek at Horsham for a few days. He made the specific and totally unexpected proposal that I should take a year out from Bexhill and devote my time to being a deacon in Horsham He had for sometime been encouraging me to seriously consider going into the full-time stipendary ministry. He was of the opinion that I

Bishops Timothy, Andrew and Barnabas from Burma, visiting Sister Anna in August 1988.
Photo: Bexhill Observer

needed to get right away from my immediate circumstances, where my time was divided between the parish and heavy responsibilities at the Coach House. I needed space to think and pray. He felt that at the end of the year, I would know clearly what I should be doing.

This was a very attractive proposition. For a period of eight months, Sister Eva and I had already been talking about the possibility of our paths moving in different directions. She had been thinking that it might be right to move closer to one of her daughters. I knew I had a call to the priesthood. Although John had given me marvellous opportunities as a deacon, he felt unable to give his support to women being priested. Perhaps Derek's suggestion was an indication that the time had come to move on.

I told Derek that two things would need to happen before I could take up his offer. First there would have to be some very clear direction and provision for Sister Eva. Secondly, there would need to be two younger people called to take up the work at the Coach House.

Imagine my surprise when I returned to Bexhill to discover that during my absence, Sister Eva had been looking through the local paper and circling round advertisements of suitable properties that would meet her needs. One property, in particular, seemed desirable. We obtained the details from the estate agent. When we looked over the house, Sister Eva was attracted to all she saw.

A few days later, I discovered that Brenda Thomas, who was preparing to be a Servant with Jesus, had already been thinking about the possibility of one day living at the Coach House with her husband, Tony.

I telephoned Derek to let him know that the two conditions needed to release me to go to Horsham seemed well on the way to being met. He said he would talk about his proposition with his churchwardens. One of them was in Germany on holiday and he would be in touch after he returned.

Meanwhile, John Cotton called to see me. Stephen Guise, our curate at St. Peter's, was due to move the following year. John asked me if I would consider becoming a full-time parish deacon for four years and move into the curate's house in April 1990!

I was in a great dilemma. Both propositions were attractive. I wrote to Derek to ask his opinion. He said that John's needs should be borne in mind but I must come to my own decision.

A few days later I was driving along Queensway to visit Sister Dorothy Ellen, who was terminally ill in the Conquest Hospital at Hastings. As I drove towards the Ridge, I noticed a small industrial unit on the righthand side of the road. To my amazement this new firm was advertising its arrival with these words, written in large letters for all to see, "This is Deacon country!"

I do not think this was a coincidence. God speaks in many different ways. The message was clear. For the time being at least, I was to stay in East Sussex.

Chapter Twentytwo

God's Secret Plans

"How unsearchable are His judgements and how inscrutable His ways!"
Romans 11:33

I had the impression that God was overseeing a kind of heavenly chessboard. A recurring feature of 1989 and 1990 was movement, both for myself and those around me. Some movements were clear and made quickly and decisively; others were revealed step by step and only taken after careful consideration.

At the beginning of July 1989, Sister Eva moved into her new home. The Servants' trustees envisaged her continuing her ministry there and giving hospitality to any overflow of guests from the Coach House.

Throughout these years, we experienced a movement of new Sisters into the Servants with Jesus. The Lord called nine Sisters to join us, which was a great encouragement.

Brenda and Tony Thomas moved into the Coach House in September. The plan was that we should share the Jerusalem life together until I moved out into the curate's house in the spring.

Eight full and energetic months followed, both in the parish and at the Coach House. The numbers of people coming to Jerusalem increased, both day visitors and house guests. Brenda offered warm hospitality to all who came.

The most worthwhile assignment for me during these months, was helping to train a lay pastoral team to work in the parish. John asked me whether I would do this. I suggested we used the Jerusalem seminar material. John agreed. About thirty of us met once a fortnight for an evening at the Coach House. In the intervening weeks, we sought to help parishioners by putting into practice the things we were learning.

During the course, we spent two weekends together at Jerusalem. Although people slept in their own homes in between learning, discussing and praying, we had meals at the Coach House. John Hind, who was still principal of the theological college at Chichester, led one of these weekends. The other weekend was conducted by David and Elsie Howell, who had a wide experience in the healing ministry. Personally I found these weekends exceptionally valuable.

Together we learnt much and were also able to encourage each other in a variety of developing ministries.

It was a great disappointment when after Easter, Brenda and Tony said they felt unable to remain at Jerusalem. The pressures and restrictions of community life did not seem right for them or their family on a continuing basis.

I was due to move into the curate's house in the not too distant future. Fairly major alterations were in progress there, particularly in the kitchen, so I decided to remain at the Coach House, away from all the chaos until these were completed. I believed that in the meantime, the Servants with Jesus would be shown what to do about Jerusalem.

Early in May, five members of the Servants with Jesus and two of their strongly supportive husbands, met for a weekend at the Coach House. The time had come for us to take stock and to see God's vision and purposes for the future. The results of our deliberations became a yardstick for our immediate decision-making and for all that has since taken place.

We talked much about the Coach House, asking ourselves questions such as, "What has God purposed it to be? What is its uniqueness? What should be taking place in Jerusalem?" We concluded that the Coach House was:

1. The mother house of the Servants with Jesus; the spiritual home of the Servants, where they come for fellowship and strengthening.
2. A centre for the renewal and unity of the life of the whole church in East Sussex and beyond; a prophetic sign of the New Jerusalem.
3. A home for one or more of the Servants with Jesus or for a Servant and her husband.
4. A place of prayer, peace, refuge, refreshment and healing for individuals and groups. It is not a holiday home but a place of Christian hospitality where people may stay and leave, invigorated and eager to do God's will and work.
5. A house of welcome providing encouragement and counsel, if desired, and teaching for those seeking to cultivate a deeper relationship with Jesus and a greater commitment to following Him.

We also spent time considering the focus for the body of the Servants with Jesus as a whole. We foresaw three developments:

1. We anticipate a period of expansion, with an increase in numbers of Servants with Jesus throughout the area.
2. We see a greater movement out from the Coach House in preaching the Gospel.
3. We see an increase in numbers coming to the Coach House for help, teaching and training in discipleship.

All these things came to pass in due course.

Another month went by and I was still living in the Coach House on my own. The alterations at the curate's house were well on their way to being completed. We needed to know God's plans for the occupation of the Coach House.

All the Bexhill Servants met every Monday morning in the prayer room to arrange and pray for the coming week. It was our practice to base our praying and thinking on the scripture passages set for the day in the Anglican lectionary. On the first Monday in June, the Old Testament reading was the story of Samuel anointing Saul. One verse seemed to leap out of the page and speak to us all. The words were Samuel's instruction to Saul after the anointing: "You shall go before me to Gilgal .... Seven days you shall wait, until I come to you and show you what you shall do." I Samuel 10:8

The Spirit gave us a united conviction that by the following Monday when we met we would know God's provision for Jerusalem.

Sunday arrived, the last day before the seven days were completed! There was still no indication of God's plans. I was due to go to Beulah in the evening to preach, for the exchange of pulpits for the week of prayer for Christian Unity. John Cotton felt strongly that I was the member of St. Peter's staff to visit Beulah on this particular occasion. During the week Neville Barnett, the minister of Beulah, telephoned. He asked if I would be willing, in addition to preaching, to be interviewed and answer some off-the-cuff questions. I agreed to do this. As the interview proceeded, Neville asked me whether there was any conflict between my commitment as a Servant with Jesus and my work in the parish. I replied, "Not usually because my main ministry as a Servant is prayer and teaching the word." I then went on to explain our present predicament at the Coach House. I asked for prayers that the right people would be found. We needed committed Christians called to take responsibility for Coach House hospitality and to be custodians of the building.

I had decided to use the Loaf vision of previous years as a part of the sermon about Christian unity. I went armed with a large visual aid to make the vision clear. I mentioned how in the Servants with Jesus and at Jerusalem, we aimed to let the Spirit bind us together in unity across all the different Christian traditions.

After the service three people mentioned how suitable Ken and Gill Wootten would be to undertake the custodianship of the Coach House. I spoke to Ken and Gill to discover that someone in the congregation had already spoken to them. I invited them to come home with me to the Coach House for coffee. I will leave Sister Gillian to share in her own words, subsequent events:

> "'You would look good in purple!' This comment was made to me on Sunday 10th June 1990 at the close of our evening service at

Beulah. The young lady who said this to me had been praying for Ken and myself for the past two months as she knew we were seeking God's will and guidance. We had recently had a terrible shock.

In April, my husband Ken and I had been given notice by our employers. The Girls' Brigade told us we would have to leave our place of work and our home at Lake House where we had been working for the last ten years as it was being sold at the end of the year. It was Maundy Thursday and a beautiful sunny day but as you can imagine our spirits were very low. My parents arrived shortly after we had received our news. My father's words to me were: 'they that honour Me I will honour them.' I Samuel 2:30. These words have stayed with us and come to mean a great deal. After we had received our news, we knew that we were wholly reliant on the Lord to lead and guide us as to the next step in our Christian lives. We had two children, Colette, who was in her final year at college before qualifying as a nursery nurse and Julian, who was about to start at Eastbourne College to do a catering course. We felt very strongly that the Lord did not want us to move out of Bexhill where we had lived for the last sixteen years, especially as Ken had recently become church secretary at Beulah. We started to look at properties in the Bexhill area as we have always felt in our Christian lives that the Lord does give us common sense and we began to push some doors. We looked at several houses, although at the time we did not have the wherewithal to buy anything. One of the houses that we looked at had a lovely flower-arranger's garden. I was very attracted to the house because flower arranging is one of my hobbies. It also had a Yorkstone fireplace in the lounge, something I had always wanted. Sister Eileen came to preach at Beulah for it was the week of prayer for Christian Unity. During the service our minister, the Rev. Neville Barnett asked her two questions. First 'how were the Servants with Jesus'?

To which she replied, 'All right'. The second question, 'How was the work going at the Coach House?' This brought the reply, 'We are waiting on God and looking for a young but mature Christian couple, who could come and run the Coach House'. Can you imagine my surprise at this comment!

The remark, 'You would look good in purple', followed by an invitation from Sister Eileen for coffee at the Coach House, made me think that perhaps God's way was opening up for us.

As we walked round the Coach House, I knew that I could see myself there. As we came to the lounge in the flat, there before my eyes was my Yorkstone fireplace! I said, 'That's my fireplace!' This was one small indication to me that perhaps God had already gone ahead of us. We chatted over a cup of coffee and as we left to go home, I said to Ken, 'I could live and work here but I would want my church to be right behind me.' I knew how some people at Beulah had been very wary of the Servants with Jesus and wondered what they were all about.

The next day while reading my Living Light I read, 'You will be called by a new name which the Lord God will bestow upon you' Isaiah 62:2. Either side of this verse, Jerusalem was mentioned and also Beulah. This is the only place in the Bible where Beulah is mentioned. Had it not been 11.20 pm, I would have telephoned Sister Eileen straightaway. The next morning, still full of excitement, I rang Sister Eileen. We had a working lunch with Sister Eileen and Sister Eva a few days later. We shared with them the things the Lord had been showing us through His word and they shared how He had been leading the Sisters. We left the Coach House agreeing that we would all continue to pray.

The next day, the Lord spoke to me through some words of Jesus in Luke 12:24, 'Consider the ravens: they neither sow nor reap, they have neither storehouse nor barn, and yet God feeds them. Of how much more value are you than birds! As I read I knew I was not to worry about the future. I also knew that God was calling me to be a Servant with Jesus and that, as a family, we should move into the Coach House.

Ken and I met with some of the trustees and the Sisters on the last Friday in June, We gave our testimonies as to how we felt God had been leading. Shortly afterwards, the trustees appointed us as custodians of the Coach House. I was anointed at a Communion service at Beulah on Sunday, 4th November for a ministry of hospitality and listening, knowing that God had called me to be a Servant with Jesus. We moved into the Coach House on 26th November 1990, ready to celebrate the eighteenth birthday of the Servants with Jesus on the 30th. I was the eighteenth Sister.

Since being at the Coach House, the Lord has never failed us. Ken waited three years for the Lord to provide a job for him and we have proved time and again, that the Lord always provides at just the right time and in His way.

The eighteenth birthday of the Servants was a very special occasion. With Ken and Sister Gillian moving into the Coach House, it was as though we had been given 'a coming of age' present. The Lord had done "exceedingly abundantly above all that we could ask or think". Not only had He provided a very committed Christian couple but two people who had ten years' experience looking after and catering for large numbers of guests.

The birthday was a day to be remembered. Bishop Peter celebrated Communion with the Sisters in the prayer room before we went to join our prayer partners and other guests. His talk helped us to put our problems into perspective. He shared how those who keep close to the Lord, are inevitably caught up into the mystery of good and evil.

Sister Marjorie Rowson had made a special birthday cake for our coming of age. Our chairman, John Bickersteth, was able to be with us, in spite of increasing physical frailty. Many friends joined in our celebrations. We gave thanks for all God had done for us in the past and for the way He was putting people in place for the future.

Chapter Twentythree

Growth and Expansion

"... neither he who plants nor he who waters is anything, but only God Who gives the growth." I Corinthians 3:7

I was surprised by the wonderful sense of freedom I experienced when I moved into the curate's house. There was a warm atmosphere and I was immediately at home.

I was there to be a parish deacon but I soon discovered that everything I did in that capacity enhanced my calling as a Servant with Jesus. In the first instance, with my own home I was free to be a 'Proverbs wife' as never before. I could entertain parishioners and those in need freely and was able to give hospitality to house guests. Secondly, I was free to pray with people and encourage them to come and share their problems. I could welcome anyone, at any time, without reference to others. The openings multiplied for sharing the Good News about Jesus and for helping people to know God as Father in a personal way. The house also lent itself well as a venue for discussion and teaching groups.

Easter Eve 1991 was for me a special time. A simple word of John's sparked off a meaningful line of thought. The servers and ministry team were rehearsing for the evening service. I was to take the deacon's role. John handed me the large Easter candle saying, "This is Eileen's candle. Other candles will be lit from her candle and taken to light the candles of the congregation." These were practical, routine instructions but God used them to point out the priority for all my future ministry. I was to bring the light of Christ into people's lives. John's words were so personally significant because my name 'Eileen' means 'light'! As all the congregation later renewed their baptismal vows, I prayed that I would be able to undertake all future responsibilities in this perspective.

The next three years were busy and rewarding. My duties in visiting the sick in their homes and nursing homes increased. I arranged fortnightly services in the Irvine Unit. I took assemblies at Ancaster House, Ancaster Gate and the Downs Infants' Schools. I enjoyed taking confirmation classes with lively and versatile members. I sometimes officiated at baptisms, weddings and funerals. A major commitment was training a second group of lay pastoral workers.

In May 1991, John was taken seriously ill. No diagnosis could be made. He became exceedingly weak. There was great concern throughout the parish and anxiety on his behalf. In these circumstances, it was not always easy to let the light go on shining brightly. John was greatly missed. He was out of action for ten weeks or so. It was a joy and great relief to everyone when he was able to take up his duties again.

It is an awesome privilege to share in people's lives and to journey with them in their joys and sorrows. During the years leading up to Easter 1994, wonderful things were happening amongst God's people at St. Peter's. Jesus Himself was clearly meeting individuals at their points of need. I found myself in situations and relationships beyond any previous imagining. These gave me insights into the priestly ministry, underlining for me my deepening conviction that God was calling me to be a priest.

Although the priestly ministry is about helping people to live abundant life, I saw that ultimately it is about preparing people to die, about helping people to face death positively, as a homecoming. I have therefore decided to write about three fellow travellers. In the providence of God, they helped me to draw this conclusion, each of them having already reached their own homecoming.

One of these was Steve, a perceptive, broken young man in his early thirties, with a passion for helping the deprived. In his own great unhappiness, God spoke to him plainly. His older sister and close confidant had died. Although he was not in the habit of attending church, in his grief he had adopted the practice of visiting churches to sit and think. On one such occasion, a picture of bread and wine on the Communion table formed in his mind. He had a strong conviction and desire to partake. He knew this was not possible until he committed himself as a Christian and was baptised. Some days later he went into St. Peter's church. One of the wardens on watch duty asked if she could help in any way. "I want to be baptised" was the reply.

As I was about to start confirmation classes, John put me in touch with Steve. The first time we met, he shared his experience in the church. He wanted to know if it had been God speaking to him. He also thought God might be calling him to be a priest. He had an intense ambition to help the marginalised. He wondered whether the best way of doing this was by becoming a priest and forming a small informal community.

I quickly realised that Steve was a most unusual young man, whose needs would not be fully met in a routine confirmation class. John agreed that it would be best for Steve to prepare for baptism and confirmation on his own. He was baptised at the family Eucharist on the first Sunday in Advent. After his baptism he wanted literally to shout for joy so he left the church immediately for fear of disturbing the congregation! A fortnight later several members of St. Peter's accompanied us to St. Augustine's for his confirmation. I was able to introduce Steve to Bishop Peter after the service, as a young man who might have a vocation to the priesthood or the religious life. Bishop Peter suggested he made an appointment to see him within the next few weeks.

The following day, Steve turned up on my doorstep at 7.30 am. He said he needed to talk to me and asked if he could come with me to the early Communion service. I invited him to come back to breakfast. I was astonished by what he had to say. He had woken early and read his Bible when God spoke to him about leading a disciplined life in preparation for the future. It was impossible for him to do this in his present circumstances. He thought that God had been preparing a place for him to live in the curate's house so that I could teach him to be disciplined!

Many things went though my mind. Predominant was the thought that if I said "No", the rejection would be disastrous after all the joy of the baptism and confirmation. I said, "Yes, but only until you have seen Bishop Peter. He must decide whether that is right for you on a more permanent basis."

Early in January, Steve met with Bishop Peter. He was very encouraging, telling Steve he was truly 'Christ's man'. Bishop Peter considered it right for Steve to remain in the curate's house until he discovered God's next step.

The following two years were demanding, full and challenging. I trust that Steve learnt the things he needed to learn. I certainly learnt many new things about life and deprivation.

Steve asked if he could convert one of the small upstairs rooms into a prayer room. He set to work, creating a peaceful focal point in a busy house.

When Steve first moved in, he was working as a carer at St. Mary's, a school for disabled children and those with learning difficulties. He later made a move to the St. Nicholas Fellowship in St. Leonards, to look after homeless teenagers. I never ceased to wonder at his ingenuity and ability to communicate.

Steve worked hard at theological studies. Under the direction of a tutor at Lewes, he wrote some excellent essays and showed a remarkable grasp of the difficult books he read. I arranged for him to visit Chichester Theological College. He did not feel the college environment was right for him. In fact he eventually came to the conclusion that all institutional training on offer was not what he needed. He applied for a post as a layworker amongst young people in a tough London parish. He was interviewed and shortlisted but not offered the post. He was bitterly disappointed and felt rejected by the church.

Steve perhaps over-reacted but, in some measure, his sense of rejection was justified. His experience raised a number of questions in my own mind. Was the church socially too conventional? Was the church so middle class in its orientation and leadership that others felt uncomfortable in her ranks? Was the church too narrow in its concept of suitable qualifications for the priesthood? Were these some of the reasons the church was so often out of touch and failing to communicate?

In due course, Steve moved to St. Leonards. He became actively involved in social work and started to train as a social worker. Sadly three years later, he collapsed and died suddenly while playing football. John invited me to preach at his funeral. This was a deeply moving occasion. The church was full mainly with people in their twenties and thirties. I have never seen a larger crowd at St. Peter's for a funeral even for well-known civic dignitaries. Two hundred or so followed on to the cemetery. I then went on to a reception at the Sidley cricket club. I mingled with numbers of young people. It was quite clear that Steve had touched many lives with love and understanding. Some said they did not know what they were going to do without him. It was obvious to me that, although Steve had not been ordained as a priest, he had been engaged in a priestly work. Possibly he had helped to mend more broken lives and given more people hope than many in the ordained ministry?

Steve reached his potential in his comparatively short life. From the experience of his own wounds and sufferings, he was able to bring healing to others. I know Steve himself will have rejoiced at his homecoming. Many lost a wonderful friend. I felt I lost a son.

During the autumn of 1992, I met Peter for the first time. I went to his home to arrange his wife's funeral. Never have I met anyone in such despair and with so little hope. He could not think of a single thing he would like at his wife's funeral. He sat and cried through our whole meeting. He said he had no belief in a future. He did not know where Ida had gone; she probably did not exist anymore and he did not know how he could live without her. Please would I decide what should be done at the funeral and do whatever I thought suitable. He told me very little about Ida except that she had been a keen flower-arranger and entered international competitions.

A few days after the funeral I received a short 'thank-you ' letter, containing these words, "I am sure, if the better place exists, Ida is now busy arranging heavenly flowers."

To my surprise Peter appeared at the parish Eucharist the following Sunday. He continued to come every Sunday. He usually sat behind a pillar. Later he told me he wept through the services. After the service, he would join parishioners in the community centre for coffee. Gradually he became the life and soul of the party. He had been a salesman in his secular work and possessed outstanding gifts of humour and communication. With a considerable amount of hesitancy, he agreed to join a confirmation class in the autumn of 1994, on the understanding that he could withdraw at any point. The group consisted of three men. It was one of the liveliest groups I have ever taken.

After Peter's confirmation, he became a personal friend. We started to entertain parishioners and others to meals together. This added a whole new dimension to my life and ministry.

Peter had an older brother, George, who had been a Christian for about sixty years and an active member of St. Martin's in the Bull Ring, Birmingham. Peter sent him a parish magazine which listed those who had been confirmed. Three weeks after the confirmation, I received a letter from George who was so thrilled that Peter had come to faith for he had prayed for him for many years. George wrote, "The confirming of Peter came as a surprise and a shock and now I know for certain that all things are possible with God. When I'm having my quiet time, I shall ask the Lord to keep a strong hold on His new convert." Four months later George, who was also a widower, joined Peter in his home. Together they were a strong team, giving warm hospitality, dispensing Christian love and full of fun. Peter died suddenly nearly a year later. He left a great gap in our lives. We were sad but at the same time we could rejoice because we knew he was ready for his homecoming.

The third person I want to mention is Dorothy, a Jewess in her early eighties, living in one of the local residential homes. She had telephoned John and asked if one of the clergy could visit her. John asked me to go. I was surprised and delighted by my visit. Dorothy was a physically frail lady but with an exceptionally enquiring and alert mind. After she had thanked me for coming, she said, "I am a Jewess and I want to die a Christian. Can you help me? I have prayed all my life but I cannot understand what is meant by Jesus being the Son of God."

I suggested she read a short passage from St. John's Gospel each day. I explained the Gospel was written by a Jewish Christian to help people to know Jesus as God's Son. I thought she might be too frail to come out in the evenings to join my boisterous class, so suggested I would visit her each week to talk over any new discoveries and answer questions. Before we reached the end of the first chapter, the Holy Spirit had helped her to understand the heart of the Gospel. It was when we reached John the Baptist's words about Jesus that light dawned: "Behold, the Lamb of God, Who takes away the sin of the world." John 1:29. She already knew how the blood of the Passover lambs protected the Israelites in Egypt from judgement of death and delivered from slavery. She saw so clearly that Jesus was the true Passover Lamb, who protected from death and the consequences of sin and delivered from being a slave to human weakness.

Dorothy was excited by this revelation and eager to join the confirmation group. She greatly enriched our discussions and, with a lovely sense of humour, brought joy to us all.

She was baptised and confirmed at the same time as Peter. Neither of them was able to kneel so they went forward together to be confirmed. As deacon, I was standing very close to them and to Bishop Eric, with the anointing oil. When the Bishop laid hands on them, the power of the Holy Spirit was so strong that His presence was tangible. Dorothy seemed to be drunk with the Spirit like the first disciples on the day of Pentecost. Peter and Eddy, one of the other confirmation candidates, had to support her to the reception after the service. To use the words of St. Peter, she was filled with "unutterable and exalted joy". I Peter 1:8. She retained her joy until she died six months later.

We used words from the Nunc Dimittis as the central theme for Dorothy's funeral service: "Lord, now lettest Thou Thy servant depart in peace, according to Thy word; for mine eyes have seen Thy salvation...." Luke 2:29-30. After the service Peter, George and I gave hospitality to some of Dorothy's friends and Jewish nephews and nieces. They were intrigued by Dorothy's new and vital faith. They asked many questions and thanked us for taking such a Jewish funeral!

As my personal ministry grew and expanded so the Servants with Jesus' ministry at Jerusalem grew and developed. Sister Gillian, supported by her husband Ken, gave hospitality to an ever-increasing number of visitors. She gave a listening ear to those who needed to talk and unburden themselves. She provided for numerous and varied church groups coming for study, prayer, conference or quiet days. Most of these groups were from East Sussex churches and visited us on Saturdays.

The Coach House remained open on weekdays for casual visitors and for those needing peace and quiet. Jerusalem seminars continued and we could see that God was preparing people for a wide variety of ministries. It was obvious that Sister Gillian needed more practical help if the Coach House was to reach its fullest potential. Also we were being asked many questions about the ministry of the Servants with Jesus.

We therefore arranged to have a day with the Servants in the Manor Barn in May 1991 to share our vision for the future. It was an inspiring day of worship, prayer for East Sussex and commitment. This was followed by three years of growth and development.

During this period fourteen new Sisters were called and commissioned as Servants with Jesus. Some new Seventies joined the team to help Sister Gillian with the work at the Coach House.

Another helpful development was the formation of a small group of men to help and support us. This was the inspiration of Ken Wootten. He writes, "In the summer of 1992, the Lord spoke to me about forming a men's fellowship closely linked to the Servants with Jesus. After much prayer, thought and discussion with Keith Adlam and Peter Ewen, we decided to form a fellowship of men who already had connections with the Servants with Jesus. The scripture the Lord gave us was from a passage in the book of Proverbs, important to the Servants. It speaks of men sitting at the gate of the city. Proverbs 31:23. So a group known as 'Men at the Gate* came into being to support and pray for the work of the Sisters."

With the expansion of the Servants with Jesus, it was important to plan for the future. With this in mind, three younger Servants – Sisters Cynthia Jeffrey, Anne Eden and Joan Adlam – were invited to join Sister Eva and myself on the Oversight. They took on their new responsibilities at our nineteenth anniversary in November 1991.

A year later they were helping us to decide whether or not to lease the Manor Barn. Our work was expanding rapidly and we had always felt that the whole Manor site should be preserved as a peaceful area. In January 1993, an advertisement appeared in the local press, inviting applications to lease the property.

At the time, we had what for us was an unusually large reserve of finances. We therefore felt it right to knock on this door and submit an application. Much effort was put into this project. One Saturday in April, we arranged a day in the Manor Barn for our prayer partners and supporters. We wanted them to be well informed so that they could pray with understanding.

Providentially, our application was unsuccessful. Rother District Council offered the lease to a commercial enterprise which eventually withdrew. This was because more restoration work was needed than anticipated -about £70,000! The energies we had put into the application, were later to prove worthwhile. Our expressed interest in the Manor site was to lead, in due course, to us being able to purchase the freehold of the Coach House.

Very sadly John Bickersteth was not with us when we celebrated our nineteenth anniversary. He had died the previous month after a long and exhausting illness. He was greatly missed by the Servants, not just as our chairman of trustees, but for the tremendous personal encouragement he gave to us all. In much physical weakness, he continued to care and pray for many people and the interests of the Kingdom of God. His strong Christian faith in the face of death was a wonderful inspiration. To the end of his life, he was convinced that the Lord was preparing the church in East Sussex for Revival.

John encouraged those who had shared this conviction to continue in that expectation. Shortly before he died, he wrote to me inviting me to join a group of Christian leaders, who had been meeting monthly at Ashburnham to pray and prepare for Revival. We later talked about this proposition on the telephone. In passing, I commented on how tired I was feeling. His response was, "You still have another forty years to do!" It seemed that I had no choice but to join the group, especially as John Cotton encouraged me to do so, inspite of my duties at St. Peter's.

The four years I spent as a full-time parish deacon were very rewarding. I shall always be grateful to John Cotton for making them possible. Overshadowing this whole period, was the issue of women being priested which I shall write about in the next chapter.

Chapter Twentyfour

Journey into Priesthood

My times are in Thy hand. Psalm 31.15

"It really does seem God is calling you to be a priest. You will have a very tough time. You must feel free to come and see me whenever you need to".

These were Father Derek Allen's words to me in January 1991. He was still my spiritual director. At his suggestion, we had set aside a whole afternoon to talk. He wanted to discern whether I was being called to the priesthood. It was a solemn time. We talked through my whole spiritual journey and calling to date. As we both stood for me to leave, he gave me a special blessing for protection which I can best describe as enfolding me in the embrace of God. He was very definite that he thought I had priestly qualities and a calling.

Two weeks later Father Derek died suddenly. At his funeral, his presence seemed very, very close especially during the consecration prayers. When I returned home, God's presence filled the house. It was as though Father Derek's spiritual presence was there too. I sat down and took up a notebook to write. A train of thought went clearly through my mind. As the words formed, I could remember Father Derek's voice so clearly that it seemed he himself was speaking.

"Dear Eileen, do not grieve so! The pain you have suffered will make you a means of blessing to God's people. I will pray for you. You are not alone. The whole company of heaven surrounds you and waits to greet you when your work is done .... Trust your soul to His peace and your body to His loving embrace. Dear Eileen, you will find all the strength you need in Jesus, our Saviour and Lord".

Those last days in January were awe-inspiring. There was no choice. I had to follow the path towards priesthood. To refuse would have been to destroy my inner integrity. I resolved that in the months ahead, I would never initiate discussions with members of St. Peter's about the pros and cons for women being priested. I would only give personal testimony to my calling in response to people's questionings.

In February, there was a meeting of the deanery synod to debate the issue of the priesting of women. Father Derek was to have been the speaker giving arguments against. When we met in January he suggested that I should be ready to give brief testimony to my calling during the open discussion. I shared this with Denis Rankin, our rural dean. He decided it was right for me to do this. After the meeting had finished, I had a number of interesting and worthwhile conversations.

On Palm Sunday, I was due to preach at Evensong. While I was preparing, a meditation began to flow through my mind. It portrayed the experiences and thoughts of the Lord as He made His way to Jerusalem and the Cross. It was as though He was preparing some of us to share in His sufferings as we stepped out in obedience with Him. For me these insights were most significant:

> "I looked for love –
> > but I found pain,
> > the loneliness of being shunned,
> > for One Who was the Son of God.
>
> I looked for love –
> > but envy found.
> > When people turned to Me in joy,
> > the fires of envy flamed and raged.
> > In passion they destroyed and burned.
>
> I looked for love -
> > and coldness knew,
> > for fear of getting too involved,
> > with One Who seemed far too extreme,
> > might even rock the Ark of God!
>
> I looked for love –
> > but judgement came.
> > The critics soon disturbed My peace.
> > My Spirit broke into despair,
> > until great darkness touched My Soul.

I looked for love –
>   but sorrow found,
>   the weeping of a broken heart.
>   My friends denied they owned My Name;
>   betrayed, deserted, left alone!

I looked for love –
>   but found a Cross
>   the instrument of hate and shame.
>   So scorned by men, was left to die,
>   by those whom I had thought My friends.

I gave My love!
>   My Father blessed!
>   Forgiveness was outpoured in Blood!
>   The Spirit breathed and cast out fear,:
>   as Love enfolded man and God."

Throughout the difficult years of uncertainty, Derek Tansill was a tower of strength. He made himself readily available to talk when I needed to and encouraged me to persist in my calling. He gave me timely invitations to Horsham, sometimes to take part in ministry. He consistently was unable to recommend that I gave up the idea of being priested but urged me to be patient.

By May, it was time for parishes and deaneries to express their views about women's ordination. This was for the benefit of diocesan representatives who were preparing for the debate in the general synod which was to take place in November 1992.

At our parish discussion, only three members of the parochial church council voted against. At the deanery synod a week later, held at St. Augustine's, the ordination of women was rejected by a small majority. As the rural dean read the results, there was a power cut and all the lights went out. There was a most extraordinary atmosphere. For some, it seemed symbolic of the Spirit being quenched. The sequence of events was so strange. Only the roads in the immediate area of St. Augustine's were in darkness. When we left the meeting, the rest of Bexhill, Cooden and Little Common were still in the light!

Throughout the Chichester diocese, opposition to the ordination of women was considerable. At the parish and pastoral level, I needed to be free to give the absolution and celebrate communion in the homes of parishioners. There were times when the ministry I was able to offer was incomplete, particularly when dealing with sickness and the dying. The struggle ahead to be priested, promised to be difficult. My parents were approaching their nineties and were in need of more frequent visits. The attitude towards women's ordination in the Chelmsford diocese was much more favourable. I seriously considered moving to Chelmsford, thinking it might be easier for everyone if I removed myself from the local scene. However, this course of action presented me with a problem. Due to my earlier calling to East Sussex, I did not feel I could easily leave the area. It did occur to me that if I was ordained elsewhere, I might be able to return to East Sussex at a later date.

While I was pondering about this whole situation, guidance came from an unexpected direction. After John Bickersteth's death, Brian Betts, who had succeeded John as the director of Ashburnham, took over the leadership of John's group of East Sussex ministers. In the spring of 1992, two other groups of East Sussex leaders approached Brian. They too had been praying for Revival and had decided in future to meet together. They asked Brian if Ashburnham Place could be their venue. Brian told them about his own group.

The result was a preliminary meeting of the three groups on 18th June 1992 at Ashburnham. Only those who had been members of one of the original groups attended this initial meeting. The gathering began with free worship and prayer. During this time, Dennis Nolan, the minister of Battle Baptist church, had a threefold prayer vision about the church of God in East Sussex.

Dennis shared what he had seen with the three dozen or so leaders present. We came from varied church backgrounds. First he had seen a number of very deep trenches, rather like the trenches in the Great War. They were so deep that the people in them had no idea what was going on in the other trenches. Rain was falling gently and people were being refreshed. In the second part of the vision, the trenches were gradually filling with water until they were overflowing and disappearing in a flood. The people in the trenches had the choice either to rise with the waters or to stay in the trenches and drown. In the third picture, the flood turned into a tide with large waves. There were surfers standing on surfboards, riding with the tide. "The only person I can recognise," said Dennis, "is Sister Eileen!" Everyone laughed.

The vision was weighed. It was agreed that the trenches represented the state of the church in East Sussex at that time. Different church traditions were so entrenched in their own concerns and activities that they were not aware that God was blessing other Christians too. The second picture indicated that the Spirit would continue to be poured out in blessing. Those who responded to all God was doing, would be joined together in a wonderful unity. Those who resisted God's blessings would stay in their spiritual trenches and spiritually drown. The surfers were those who recognised God's spiritual waves. As they saw what God was doing, they were eager to move with Him in Revival.

No one thought to interpret why I was in the vision on a surf board! The message though was very clear to me. However hard the going, I had to stay in East Sussex.

Later I telephoned Dennis to ask him if he himself was inside or outside the vision. "Inside," he said, "I was on a surfboard too. There were a number of us standing and holding hands down the line to help keep our balance. I looked to see if I could recognise anyone. I saw you several places along on the right." What we did not know at the time was that three years on Dennis would become the chairman of trustees to the Servants with Jesus.

Five months later, general synod agreed to the ordination of women to the priesthood. The same evening Bishop Ian Cundy, our new bishop, had planned to visit Battle and Bexhill deanery to give an address to the synod at St. Peter's. He gave a sensitive talk making it clear that he supported women's ordination. He showed how pleased he was that women students he had known in the past at Durham would now be able to fulfil their callings.

On Candlemas 1993, I went to visit Bishop Ian with Michael Townroe. This was Michael's suggestion. He felt it important that Bishop Ian knew about my work at the Grammar School and subsequent call to East Sussex and the Servants with Jesus. He wished to accompany me as my ex-chairman of governors and ex-rector. Bishop Ian was enthusiastic in his response to the things we shared. He said he would like to visit the Coach House and that he had a number of ideas about a possible future for me. All this was most encouraging. It was a great disappointment therefore when a year later, he was unable to fulfil any of the propositions he had in mind.

15th May 1994, was the date fixed for the ordination of the first women priests in the Chichester diocese. Those hoping to be ordained had to go through a discernment process. This involved an interview with a priest sympathetic towards women's ordination, to test our priestly callings. My interview took place with Andrew Robinson, the chaplain of Sussex University. I made my way to Falmer on a very snowy day. I had a sense of peace and the Lord's presence on the icy roads and throughout the whole day. I enjoyed the interview and felt relaxed. I was recommended as having a strong call to the priesthood.

Imagine my surprise and disappointment when a few days later, Bishop Ian asked me to visit him with Derek Tansill. He told us that it was not possible for me to minister as a priest at St. Peter's but he wanted me to remain there as a non-stipendary deacon to support John. I asked him if it would be possible for him to look for another opening where I would soon be able to serve as a priest, bearing in mind my age and that the number of years left to serve was limited.

Bishop Ian asked me to visit him again in Holy Week. He told me he had been unable to find anywhere for me to go. He informed me that, although my assessment had been positive, my papers were not being forwarded to Bishop David Wilcox for ordination. I was to remain at St. Peter's as a deacon.

Spiritually, emotionally and intellectually this situation did not seem to make sense. It seemed incomprehensible to me that my calling could have been so thoroughly tested and that no opening could be found for its fulfilment. I was devastated and filled with inner pain and grief.

Without the Lord's special grace, I would not have managed to take part in the good Friday and Easter services. It was at the Good Friday ante-Communion service, as John and I began to say the Lord's Prayer together, that I nearly broke down. I recovered sufficiently to minister the Cup but after the service, stayed in the vestry on my own and wept.

On Easter Saturday, I received a letter from Bishop Ian, confirming our earlier conversation. This was the culmination of several difficult and stressful months for all of us involved in the situation. There was no point in apportioning blame. We were all seeking to do God's will as we understood it and to preserve our inner integrity. Perhaps for each of us, it was a growing experience. A cause for much thanksgiving was that throughout the whole process, my fellowship and friendship with John Cotton remained intact. We knew that true unity in Christ is something much bigger than agreement to theological detail.

The Lord made wonderful provision for me at this time to help me carry on and to keep sane. One was a beautiful bungalow where I could make a new home, when I moved out of the curate's house at the end of April. Another gift was my growing friendship with Peter. He was marvellous. His humour and resourcefulness brought joy, happiness and healing. I understand that an inquisitive parishioner was bold enough to ask him about our relationship. He replied, "I am Sister Eileen's chaplain. Don't you know?!"

Chapter Twentyfive

Fulfilment

"Behold, I have set before you an open door, which no one is able to shut."
Revelation 3:88

"Why can't everyone be happy?"

I often heard my mother make this comment. She devoted her life to making others happy. It was a great disappointment to her when those around her were unhappy and hurting.

I think I share something of her outlook. After the sense of rejection caused by the delay of ordination, I was determined to be positive. I knew I was to live in the reality of Jesus' promise that no man could take away the joy of His followers. I knew too that God had called me to be a priest. The call came from God Himself and must therefore be unchanging and sure. He would open a door for His calling to be fulfilled.

Meanwhile, I resolved to enjoy the company and fellowship of His people. I would continue to take every opportunity to share the word of God. With Peter's help and a new home, I would offer more and more hospitality to parishioners and friends. A year of healing and entering into a new wholeness and happiness followed this decision.

John Cotton came to bless my new home early in April 1994. Peter and his brother George, who was staying with him for a short holiday, helped prepare refreshments for the happy celebration that followed.

After George returned to Birmingham, Peter suggested we held a 'Get to Know' coffee morning in the garden and invite all the neighbours who lived in the Briary to join us. I had never done such a thing. Peter assured me, with his saleman's expertise, that it would be a great success and it was. Thirty-five people came. Several who had never spoken to each other before, began to communicate. The whole event proved a wonderful way of being in touch with people. A few weeks later, we organised a barbecue. Sixty-five neighbours and friends spent an enjoyable evening together.

In July, George moved from Birmingham to live with Peter. Together we entertained many guests, sometimes in Peter and George's home, sometimes in mine. We also enjoyed the hospitality of others. This was a time of inner healing for all of us. Peter surfaced gradually from his deep grief. His sense of humour and fun returned to the great blessing of others.

Uppermost in George's perception of Christian discipleship was the importance of daily living the abundant life. Getting to know so many new friends gave him much joy and satisfaction. Step by step, I realised that I too was being healed from inner wounds left by the stresses and tensions of recent years.

Our social life had a very positive effect on my pastoral ministry. I found myself in touch with an ever-increasing circle of people. Also at this time, the number of opportunities to pray with the sick and distressed multiplied. I discovered it was often beneficial to use anointing with oil.

Throughout this period, two threads of events culminated in the fulfilment of two cherished aspirations. The first was ordination; the second was the purchase of the Coach House freehold by the Servants with Jesus. These two threads were interwoven with three threads of personal bereavement in the summer of 1995. So many different happenings occurred in a short space of time and so much interweaving of threads that the tapestry pattern, of which Michael Townroe had spoken in earlier years, began to take shape.

The final thread towards ordination began with a conversation with John Cotton in July 1994. He seemed to recognise that I had a strong call to become a priest and suggested that I renewed my contact with Bishop Ian. After much thought, I decided to wait until the September chapter meeting when Bishop Ian was due to visit us. If there was a suitable opportunity to speak to him, I would raise the matter of ordination. It was wonderfully easy to do this because at the end of the meeting, he approached me to ask how I was. As a result, he arranged to see me in October.

Before keeping this appointment, I had a God-given meeting with Marianne Gamester in Sainsbury's. I had known Marianne and her husband, Peter, for some years. I had not seen them for several months so invited them to lunch. Peter had retired the previous year as rector of St. Mark's Little Common. During lunch he shared how the new rector, John Edmondson, was in great need of help. Peter, also knew that John was in favour of women's ordination. He wondered whether there might be an opening for me to serve as a priest in Little Common.

My visit to Bishop Ian was positive and helpful. On arrival it was reassuring to hear him say that he believed I had a call to be a priest. I shared with him, my conversation with Peter Gamester and he agreed to knock on the St. Mark's door. I later received a letter from Bishop Ian to say that John Edmondson was prepared to explore with his churchwardens the possibility of me helping in the parish.

In December, John Edmondson telephoned to say that Bishop Ian was suggesting I went to St. Mark's during Lent, with a view to being ordained in June. He himself was writing to all the parochial church council members asking them to pray. They would make a decision at their next meeting on 17th January. Late that evening John telephoned to say that the church council had voted by a large majority to give me an invitation to serve in the parish.

On my last Sunday at St. Peter's in March 1995, John Cotton asked me to preach at the parish Eucharist and at Evensong. I felt I was given special grace and strength to do this with poise and purpose. I was wonderfully supported by the love expressed by so many of the Lord's people. John invited Michael Townroe to join with him in celebrating Communion which was a lovely touch of warmth and love. The same afternoon a parish farewell tea party was arranged. Here I had the opportunity to say "Goodbye!" and to thank many friends for their prayers and support over the years.

Leaving St. Peter's was a massive bereavement experience. I was due to start at St. Mark's a fortnight later. The intervening Sunday had a kind of limbo feel about it. In the early morning, I had a strange feeling of being cut off from others as though I did not belong anywhere. The thought came to me that this is how so many feel – separated from their fellow human beings. For some, this pain is intensified by a feeling of isolation and alienation from God. I saw more than ever before the importance of getting involved closely with all kinds of people and sharing in their lives, their hopes, their fears as Jesus did. As a priest there would be no short cut if others were to come to know the love of God.

There were two encouraging happenings on that first Sunday away from St. Peter's. One was the arrival just before lunch, of Carl Mullineux, one of St. Peter's lay pastoral team. He came with a gift of two photograph albums full of pictures of many of my St. Peter's friends which he had taken at the tea party the previous week. The other was an inspiring visit to Marlis Bickersteth, John's widow. Marlis invited me to supper. We had an enjoyable evening sharing many things about the past, the present and hopes for the future of Ashburnham, the Servants with Jesus and the Lord's work in East Sussex. The vision of God moving in Revival in East Sussex was strengthened and renewed.

I met with John Edmondson on the Saturday before my commissioning at St. Mark's. He said he wanted our future ministry to be joyful, positive and prosperous. I could identify with these sentiments wholeheartedly.

Throughout the next day, I received an overwhelming welcome at St. Mark's. The first moving touch was a chrysanthemum plant from Patrick Bodle, the verger, when I arrived to assist John at the early Communion service. I had got to know Patrick over the years. In the past he had brought St. Mark's people to the Coach House to take part in Jerusalem seminars. This had created a special bond between Patrick and the Servants with Jesus. At the evening service of Commissioning, John said he hoped I would be at St. Mark's for many years and prayed for joy, prosperity and peace. I went home feeling very uplifted.

The first few weeks at St. Mark's were tremendously happy in spite of the enormous effort I had to make to get to know many new faces and names. The only thing that clouded this time was constant delays in the announcement of the date for ordination. John made numerous unsuccessful enquiries. We needed to make plans for parishioners and friends to be with us on that day. Also my family and friends wanted to support me with informed prayer and when possible, with their presence. As things worked out, Peter and both my parents died within four weeks of each other, not knowing the date fixed for my ordination.

Peter died suddenly on the first Saturday in June from a heart attack. Hearing the news, friends from St. Peter's came the next day to the evening service at St. Mark's to support me. John Cotton invited me to St. Peter's to preach at Peter's funeral. Derek Tansill telephoned to say I must let others help me in my bereavement. This was a word of advice that I heeded. Michael Townroe telephoned and I shared with him how I still did not know the day for ordination. This was difficult because of all that had to be done in connection with Peter's death. I knew too that an interview was to be arranged with the ordaining bishop before ordination could take place.

Michael took it upon himself to telephone Bishop David Wilcox, who was to take the ordination service. Bishop David was very helpful. He said that the ordination was to take place on 9th July. He would like to see me on 14th June, the day after Peter's funeral. This proved to be a providential timing as on 15th June, I was called to Chelmsford to my father, who was dying.

God's provision and timing of everything was perfect and quite extraordinary. John Edmondson had worked in the Guildford diocese before coming to St. Mark's and knew Bishop David. He offered to drive me to Guildford. John and his wife, Jill, cared for me lovingly throughout the day which helped me to relax and get through the day without any anxieties. To my great delight, Bishop David accepted me for ordination and I was able to look forward to the future positively.

It was wonderful to have had this day of oasis before receiving the news the next morning by telephone about my father. Half an hour later, George, his friend John Hayward and I set out for the burial of Peter's ashes in the garden of remembrance at St. Peter's. After the short service George and John prayed with me and sent me on my journey to Chelmsford. I was able to be with my father for three hours before he died peacefully in the evening.

I returned to Bexhill after my father's funeral with just over a fortnight to go before my ordination. There were many cards and letters of sympathy waiting for me with promises of people's prayers. I received a strengthening letter from Bishop Peter who had heard of my news. "I am sure that your priesting will make lots of difference both in the parish and with the Sisters and I hope that the pain of real priesthood won't be too much for you with all else you are bearing."

Eight days later, my brother Selwyn telephoned to say that my mother had died. He took charge of affairs. He said he would come from Scotland and arrange the funeral and deal with all the business. I was to concentrate on getting ready for ordination. It was a great relief having Selwyn take the mam responsibility for everything. There was however a lovely touch in the Lord's timing of things. A few days before I was due to go to the ordination retreat, Geoffrey Roper, my mother's minister, came to Eastbourne for a national conference of United Reformed ministers. I was able to meet him and talk over suggestions for my mother's funeral. I particularly wanted to share with him some verses my mother had written expressing her faith We decided that I should read these at the funeral service:

> "Are you sad or feeling lonely?
> Are you weary, ill at ease?
> Stand and listen, look around you.
> Jesus of Nazareth passeth by.
>
> Are you worried, always anxious
> Of the things that are to be?
> Cease to worry, look around you
> Jesus of Nazareth passeth by.
>
> You must stop and call upon Him.
> Ask Him what you ought to do.
> Don't go on your way without Him.
> Jesus of Nazareth passeth by.
>
> When you wake up in the morning.
> Stay and ponder for a while
> Don't rush out before you listen.
> Jesus of Nazareth passeth by.
>
> Then go out to do your duty.
> Ask Him to be by your side.
> No more need for fear or worry.
> Jesus of Nazareth walks with you."

Immediately before the ordination retreat, I went to St. Andrew's, Burgess Hill, for the ordination rehearsal. On the way back to Bexhill, I visited Derek Tansill at Horsham. He gave me a copy of Henri Nouwen's book, 'The Return of the Prodigal Son' to read at the retreat. This book has since had a profound effect on my thinking and ministry.

The three days of retreat provided a very necessary space for reflection and for coming to terms with all that had been happening. The Rev. Barry Preece led our thoughts interspersing sensitive meditations with music and poetry It was exactly what I needed.

The ordination service was a time of moving celebration and fulfilment. Many friends were there to pray and support me on a very hot summer's day It was wonderful that my brother was able to be at the service. Normally he would have been in Scotland and it would have been difficult for him to be present. Peter and my parents were not able to be with us in the flesh but, as we celebrated Communion together, it seemed they were very much with us in spirit.

The next day was the monthly meeting of all the Servants with Jesus at the Coach House. We were able to celebrate Communion together at our Jerusalem with much rejoicing.

Alongside the unfolding of events which led to ordination, ran a second thread leading to the purchase of the Coach House freehold. Our application to lease the Manor Barn in 1993 had been unsuccessful. The successful tenderers had withdrawn so Rother District Council had retained responsibility for the maintenance and hiring of the Barn. Approximately a year later, I was approached by a Rother District Council official who asked, "Were the Servants with Jesus still interested in leasing the Manor Barn? The Council could not afford the upkeep. They wanted to maintain a community spirit in the Old Town. They knew we were concerned about the preservation of the whole area. If we leased the Barn, we could help to do this." My response to this was, "In four years' time, our lease on the Coach House runs out. If this is not renewed, we will have no use for the Manor Barn. However, we might be interested in purchasing the freehold of the Coach House!"

Some weeks later, Mr. Hampton, one of the Council's officials, visited us and encouraged us to write officially to Mr. David Powell, the chief executive, expressing our interest in the purchase of the freehold. We followed his advice. In response, Mr. Hampton telephoned to say that the principle of making the freehold available for purchase was to be discussed at the next meeting of the Recreation and Tourism Committee at the end of November.

At our trustees' meeting earlier in the month, we made two unanimous decisions. One was to go for the freehold, the other to invite Dennis Nolan to become a trustee.

During our full November meeting of the Servants, a number of scripture promises encouraged us to move forward. One of these was from the book of Jeremiah, "I am watching over My Word to perform it". Jeremiah 1:12. This spoke to us because a part of the original Servants with Jesus' vision was to possess the Coach House. A few days later we heard that the councillors had given David Powell the freedom to start negotiating with us about the freehold.

We shared our plans and aims with our prayer partners. Gifts of money began to arrive for the purchase, including an anonymous gift of £10,000. These gifts were a confirmation to us that we were moving in the right direction.

Early in 1995, George Cole became our chairman of trustees and the council offered us the freehold at the purchase price of £142,500. This included a sizeable piece of derelict land to the south east of the building which had been used as a rubbish dump for the whole Manor site.

In February, the trustees had an informal meeting with David Powell. He suggested that we answered the council's letter by making an offer of £132,000 in view of the fact that repairs were needed to the drive and flint garden walls. After further negotiations, a purchase price of £132,500 was agreed.

Throughout April, gifts continued to flow from those who heard of our plans and caught the vision for a permanent Christian presence on the Manor site. Towards the end of the month, I realised that I must make freehold matters a top priority for the next few weeks. I had an inner and urgent conviction that things would move rapidly with the Council and that we must be in a position to sign all the legal documents.

We set the last Saturday of the month aside for a day of prayer at the Coach House. Some of our prayer partners and Men at the Gate joined us. Our treasurer reported that we had £50,142 in our building society account and £5,500 in promises towards the freehold. After weighing our situation carefully, we scattered to different parts of the house and Manor site to pray and seek further insights about the future. It was important that with such a large sum of money involved, we were united in believing that we were in the centre of God's will.

The extraordinary thing was that when we came together again to share our thoughts, no one spoke directly about the freehold. Most people present spoke about establishing a prayer garden. Sister Mary Stuart had a very clear vision of the wasteland behind the gardeners' yard becoming what she described as an outdoor chapel. The garden was to have flowing water and a fountain. Sister Mary was an architect and later produced an excellent working plan of the vision she had received. After others had shared complementary thoughts about creating a a garden, one of the Men at the Gate pointed out that no one had mentioned the freehold in our discussions. He continued, "If God intends that the Servants with Jesus should create this garden, they will need to own the freehold!" There was an unanimous and positive response to this comment. All present agreed that we should proceed towards the purchase of the freehold.

Throughout May, we watched and prayed with anticipation to see how God would provide. Several friends who had given strong support to the Servants over the years, gave us much encouragement. One of these was Paul Broomhall, who was a close friend of John Bickersteth. He had been chairman of the Ashburnham Christian Trust in the early days and was still an active trustee. Marlis suggested I shared our plans with Paul. I wrote to him. The next day he telephoned. In spite of his extreme physical frailty, I had a most amazing conversation with him. I shared with Paul how Rother District Council was working towards exchanging contracts at the end of June. Although there was still a large shortfall in funds, he said we should, "Press on joyfully in faith!" These were the last words he spoke to me and I shall never forget them. He was confident the Lord would release the necessary resources. Three weeks later he was advising us to sign the contract. This we did when the trustees met on 27th June sending Rother District Council a deposit of £13,250. We agreed with the council that completion date should be 14th September.

We continued to receive numerous donations. By the beginning of September, we had also been promised three interest-free loans. We were short of just over £900. During East Sussex Bible Week at Ashburnham, an offering had been made for the Servants with Jesus towards the purchase of the freehold. I understood from Dennis Nolan, who was a part of the Bible Week leadership team, that over £1,000 had been collected. A few days before completion date, I telephoned John Houghton, who was chairman of the Bible Week team, to let him know our situation. He arranged for a cheque to be sent to us immediately. We were not only able to meet the purchase price but also the cost of our solicitor's bill.

14th September 1995, traditionally Holy Cross day, was a day of great rejoicing for the Servants. We had open house all day at our Jerusalem so that our prayer partners and friends could come and rejoice with us. A part of Bexhill's Christian inheritance had been reclaimed for posterity.

The tapestry which had begun to emerge in the nineteen sixties, both in my own spiritual journey and in the life of the church in East Sussex, seemed to have reached a significant stage. I began to see more clearly that it takes a whole life time to fully realise that a power far greater than ourselves, God Himself, is at work doing the weaving and the threading.

Chapter Twentysix

Aspirations for the Future

"There is one body and one Spirit .... one Lord, one faith, one baptism, one God and Father of us all." Ephesians 4:4-6

For me the tapestry will be complete when God sends Revival to East Sussex. It is wonderfully encouraging to hear of Him blessing in other parts of the world. However, I personally will not be satisfied until Revival breaks out in 'Sussex by the sea'. I long to see hundreds of people, at present outside the church, turning to Jesus in faith.

My personal journeyings in East Sussex seemed to reach a climax in 1995. It was not only a year of fulfilment but also a year of setting free to give all my energies to occupying the 'promised land'.

What of the future? My expectancy has increased. Many have prayed. Much prayer is continuing to be offered. Although in East Sussex we are still waiting for a great outpouring of the Spirit in Revival, significant steps of preparation have been made in response to God's leading. For example, some of the cities of refuge envisaged in 1971 by John Bickersteth as part of the preparation, are in place.

The vision for the restoration of the old stableyard at Ashburnham as a place of prayer and warm centre for the people of East Sussex, has come to pass. The Servants with Jesus have purchased the freehold of the Coach House and established a place of prayer and refuge for the future in Bexhill. Since Bishop Wallace Benn came to bless the prayer garden in June 1999, many have come to pray there.

Other significant works of prayer and caring, seen in vision, are being fulfilled. In Hastings there is the Strategic Prayer Initiative, facilitated by Keith Hayden and supported by a strong team of church leaders. In Eastbourne, Sandy Medway's vision for 'People Matter' has come to fruition. A Christian centre has been established especially for equipping those who have been made redundant, are unemployed or in need of a career change. This work too is being supported and encouraged by church leaders. In Hailsham, there is an inter-church fellowship called Crosslink. Sometime ago Ron Timms had a vision for a Christian bookshop in the centre of the town. The curate had a vision for a coffee shop. These three threads came together and there is now a bookshop and a coffee shop open daily except on Sundays.

In Battle, there is the Manna House, the fulfilment of a vision given to members of Zion Baptist church. It is a place of caring outreach for people of all ages in Battle and the surrounding area.

There is every indication that God is calling and equipping a whole new generation of Christians to minister to a wide variety of needs. Sixty-one of them have been involved in an interdenominational Training Together scheme at Ashburnham. This is a two-year programme of training for Christian leadership.

The Lord has also begun to call a younger generation of Servants with Jesus. Two years ago, to her great surprise, Clare Cooper was called to be a Sister. This has given the Servants much encouragement and confidence about the future. I have asked her to tell her own story:

> "'Servants with Jesus.' The words came suddenly into my head. Clearly, firmly. And that was all.
>
> I was walking across the courtyard outside the Church of the Holy Sepulchre in Jerusalem, during a one-week pilgrimage in 1998. I had looked forward to the trip as I knew that visiting the land of Jesus would refresh me. It was wonderful to go in a boat on the Sea of Galilee, knowing Jesus had lived and worked here. After the tranquility of Galilee we journeyed to Jerusalem. There we visited the prison and pit where Jesus spent some of His last night before the crucifixion. We reflected on how He suffered. As I walked up the ancient steps to the High Priest's palace, I was thinking of how much Jesus had done for me. "What could I do in return?" I asked myself. I was deeply moved and prayed that I would do God's will whatever it was. Two days later we visited the Mount of Olives and the Garden of Gethsemane. In the afternoon we walked along the Via Dolorosa to the Church of the Holy Sepulchre. It was as we left that I heard those words in my mind: 'Servants with Jesus'. J felt at once that it was God calling me, but all I knew was that the Servants with Jesus were a group of Christian women in Bexhill who wore purple. I live in the nearby town of Hastings. I started to pray about whether this was truly God calling me. I had a slight acquaintance with Sister Marjorie Rowson, whose husband was a work colleague of my husband, and I knew she belonged to the group. I prayed that if God was indeed calling me I would see her soon after my return home. I felt safe as I only saw her once every year or two!

When I returned home I found to my surprise I would be seeing her twice within five weeks! I was anxious that the calling might be too much for me. I have three children, work part-time as a hospital doctor and at the time I was a churchwarden.

As Sister Marjorie spoke when we first met, I knew I could manage the commitment required. She offered to take me to the Coach House after Easter.

When I visited the Coach House in May, I found it was called 'Jerusalem'. Sister Marjorie explained the history of the site and I told her about my calling.

I later discovered that a central concept of the Servants was about God's people being a 'Jerusalem people'. I also discovered that each Sister must have a clear call from God. "Was my calling real?" I kept asking myself. Then God spoke to me through my daily Bible reading from Matthew 21:28-31. I knew I was like the son in this parable who said 'yes' to his father but then did not go to work in the vineyard. God showed me that I too was trying to back out. I knew I must be obedient. It was important to find out my ministry. I talked to one of my church leaders, Jan Acton, and we both agreed it was teaching. Sister Eileen had met with me in June and felt that the Lord was calling me.

We talked about my stay in Jerusalem and how while I was there I had begun to share in Jesus' sufferings, as the Sisters seek to do. I could see how the Lord had been preparing me for fellowship with them and a deeper fellowship with Himself. My husband, children and church leaders have been very supportive of my calling. On St. Luke's day 1998 I was anointed and commissioned as a Sister.

I chose a Jerusalem cross for the gold cross I wear each day." For me a more complete entering in to the reality of the Loaf vision is crucial for a greater release of the power of God in Revival. Divisions amongst Christians have quenched the Spirit and greatly damaged the effectiveness of the church. Before His death, Jesus prayed that all His disciples would be one so that the world would believe – John 17:21. He died to make this possible and God has given all authority into His hands. Therefore Jesus' prayer must be answered. It is the work of the Spirit to bring this about.

I am convinced there needs to be a deep repentance on the part of all God's people, particularly church leaders, for the grievous divisions they have allowed to take root. Church councils have struggled unsuccessfully to define a basis for unity when Jesus has already given us unity. We are rejecting His gracious gift when we behave as though our understanding of the truth is superior to that of other Christians. This was the mistake of the early Gnostic heretics! All Christian traditions have helpful insights given by the Spirit. All need to repent of arrogance in behaving as though they alone are right.

At the time I was commissioned to go out into East Sussex, I had a firm grasp of the Evangelical tradition. While I was at the Bexhill Grammar school, the Lord had intervened in so many marvellous ways that I was caught up into a powerful ongoing Pentecostal experience. I had no problems in accepting Edmund Heddle's exhortation about effective ministry being a balanced response to the word and the Spirit. This directive kept me on course and led me into a deeper appreciation of the Catholic tradition.

I was shown that the sacramental thread contained within the Catholic tradition was essential for the complete release of God's grace and power. In particular, the sacraments of baptism and Communion were vital. These were commanded by Jesus to proclaim the Gospel and to draw us closer to Him and to one another.

I have increasingly come to believe that Catholic, Evangelical and Pentecostal insights need to be equally balanced for the Kingdom life of God's people to be fully operational and effective.

Churches represented by the trenches in Dennis Nolan's vision, put a different emphasis on these three threads of tradition running through history In the vision people were being blessed in all the trenches and rising to join the floodtide of Revival together. We all need to be sensitive to what the Spirit is doing in the other trenches.

I believe it is God's intention that those who know and seek Him without reserve and long to see His purposes fulfilled, will rise together out of the trenches to flow with His flood of Revival. It will not be a case of the Pentecostal charismatics rising on their own for others to join them later. It will not be a case of everyone having to join one Catholic visible church before God can bless. It will not be a case of everyone signing up for one particular Evangelical interpretation of the scriptures, before the Gospel can be effectively proclaimed. Rather, it will be a matter of all whose hearts are totally towards God and obedient to the Spirit, who will surf on God's tide.

Epilogue

"This is the Lord's doing, it is marvellous in our eyes." Psalm 118:23

I have written of numerous wonderful things the Lord has done. I have deliberately chosen to write of light rather than darkness.

There have, however, been fierce conflicts along the way and much unnecessary hurt. These have often been caused by false accusations and misunderstandings. This has been my own personal experience and also that of other Christians around me. Those who have sought to follow the Lord in obedience have often suffered the pain of rejection. I have come to believe that such conflict is an inevitable preliminary to Revival. Our spiritual enemy contests every step of our way.

I am convinced that one of the main reasons for the delay of Revival is the quenching of the Spirit, by the failure of Christians to recognise the devices of the evil one. He is described in the scriptures as the accuser of the brethren and by Jesus as the father of lies. He is the author of confusion. We must learn not to co-operate with our spiritual enemy in these activities. I have discovered that to pray and to prepare for Revival is a costly business but glorious! In the process, we enjoy the closeness of the Lord but share in the fellowship of His sufferings.

One day during a time of particularly intense distress, a strong clear thought came into my mind, "Nothing done in love is ever wasted". These words seemed to come from God. I have held to them for encouragement and shared them with others experiencing difficulties. Love and compassion in all circumstances are the keys to God's blessing.

Our main responsibility is to watch and pray with Jesus Who is, "the same yesterday, today and forever." Hebrews 13:8. We need to pray when we are alone. We need to pray together. There is a great urgency for Christian leaders to pray regularly with other leaders in their immediate locality. This should to be a top priority if unity and understanding are to be achieved.

We should watch out for the spiritual waves God sends so that we are ready to jump instantly with Him to surf on His spiritual tide. If we are knocked off our surfboards by strong waves, we don't need to drown! Let's just be ready for the next wave!